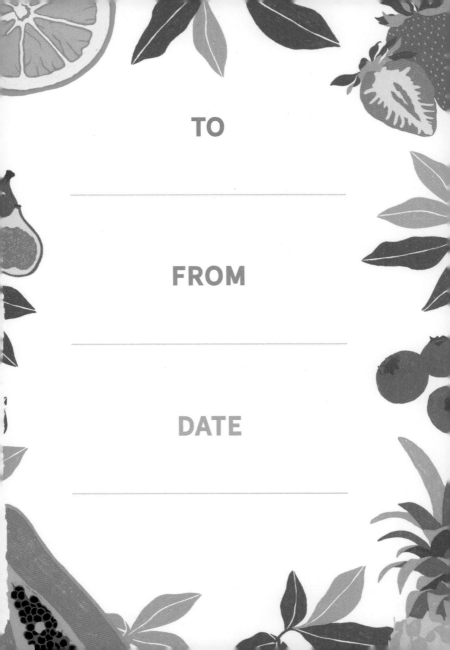

TO

_____

FROM

_____

DATE

_____

TRUE
Sweetness

GROWING IN
THE FRUIT OF
THE SPIRIT

DaySpring

LIVE YOUR FAITH

CONTENTS

INTRODUCTION

*When they saw the courage of Peter and John
and realized that they were unschooled, ordinary
men, they were astonished and they took note
that these men had been with Jesus.*

ACTS 4:13 NIV

FAMILY RESEMBLANCE

*I*t's uncanny how some families share such strong resemblance. Over the phone, sometimes their voices are indistinguishable. Or in person, the daughter laughs, gestures with her hands, and emotes with facial expressions in a way exactly like her parent. "You are just like your mother," or "I see your father in you so much," we'll say—implying that the impression the older has made on the younger is undeniable, both physically and emotionally.

We see a similar phenomenon in Scripture, concerning Jesus's disciples. As He worked out His ministry to others, Jesus spent intentional, personal, intimate time with his hand-chosen Twelve, showing and telling them the ways of the Father. Yet Jesus's calling was so countercultural, His disciples could barely grasp it. They were impatient, self-serving, and worldly, even as Jesus patiently redirected their thinking toward a kingdom mindset.

But a dramatic transformation occurred upon the descent of the Holy Spirit on the disciples of Jesus after His Ascension. Suddenly, the disciples who had faltered in their faith and speech spoke up boldly, proclaiming the gospel message. At long last, the men who had been with Jesus now looked and lived like Jesus. The resemblance was striking, and everyone took notice.

What made the difference? In a word, God—but God in a form they had not formerly known as a permanent resident inside them: the Holy Spirit. The triune God of all creation not only reigned in heaven as God the Father and walked beside them as Jesus the Son, but now He also lived *within* them as the Holy Spirit, bringing levels of understanding, power, and purpose they had never dreamed possible.

It is this same Holy Spirit, the third person of our triune God, who promises to bear His fruit in us if we receive Jesus into our lives. We, too, can have deep intimacy with God. We, too, can have the power to experience His love, guidance, and transformative presence in our lives. All this, along with the blessed hope of eternity in heaven, is possible through the power of the Holy Spirit.

True Sweetness: The Fruit of the Spirit is a simple devotional book to direct your attention to the only One able to produce the kind of fruit that makes us resemble Jesus. It is not a self-help manual or a list of to-dos, but rather an invitation to know the Holy Spirit, and to surrender to His ways through time spent in His presence. My prayer is that you will create space and time in your day to be still before the Lord. Draw near to God, and He will draw near to you. Hold to His teachings, and the truth will set you free. Just like Jesus's disciples, over time you will see the growth of His fruit in your life.

THE INHERITANCE

Peter replied, "Repent and be baptized, every one of
you, in the name of Jesus Christ for the forgiveness of
your sins. And you will receive the gift of the Holy Spirit.
The promise is for you and your children and for all who
are far off—for all whom the Lord our God will call."

ACTS 2:38-39 NIV

She hesitated as she looked over the contract. It all looked good to her, maybe even too good to be true. "So I just sign this and the property is all mine?" She turned her head toward the attorney seated next to her at the closing table, wanting his confirmation one more time.

"Yes, but that's not all," he reminded her. "In the transaction, you also agree to receive a helper for life, a person who will teach you how to manage your estate and help you run it."

This was the proposition she had not properly considered. Who was this person? Would they get along? How would this arrangement actually work?

"Don't worry," he responded to her furrowed eyebrows. "He's the most valuable part of the inheritance."

In a similar way, God the Father has given each of His children an incredible inheritance through faith in His Son, Jesus. When we sign our lives over to God, we are saying, "Yes!" to total forgiveness, adoption into His family, and the promise of eternity in heaven. But that's not all! God's great gift of salvation comes with another binding agent—the Holy Spirit! He's God's down payment of Himself, deposited directly into our hearts as proof that we have been bought by the blood of Christ *and* as a Helper who guides us in God's ways. We are literally surrounded by God's love that goes before us, behind us, beside us, and finally also inside us. To belong to Jesus means to be filled with His Spirit and the sweetness of the fruit He brings.

Father, thank You for the gift of eternal life through faith in Jesus, and thank You for giving me Your Holy Spirit as a deposit that guarantees all that is to come. Help me get to know Your Spirit better so that I can stay in step with His leading. In Jesus's name.

FIRE LIGHT

May the grace of the Lord Jesus Christ,
and the love of God, and the fellowship
of the Holy Spirit be with you all.

II CORINTHIANS 13:14 NIV

The fire crackled, burning bright against the cool night sky as the small group of lifelong friends sat in a circle around the blazing pit, soaking in the warmth and exchanging stories. It felt good, almost otherworldly, to set aside the phones and computers to simply sit outside in nature, allowing space, occasional silence, and unscripted conversation to unite their hearts even closer together. The fellowship felt like a little slice of heaven that satisfied, even for a moment, their hearts' cry for community...for love that lasts.

Even though special moments like these eventually fade like embers floating away in the night sky, God has designed each one of us for love, closeness, and connection that doesn't die. We ache for fellowship that lasts forever because God has placed eternity in our hearts. We are designed for eternal love.

For the Christian, that loving connection is far more than a fleeting emotion ignited or diminished by circumstances. For us, it is a person—namely, the Spirit of God who lives inside everyone whose faith rests in Jesus as Savior. More brilliant than any man-wrought flame, the Spirit's fire burns in our hearts with a love so intense that it shapes the way we see God and others, compelling us to open our hands and hearts to the source of such immense power and warmth. We are part of an unseen community that is destined for eternity. God has given us His Holy Spirit in our hearts to not only seal the deal of redemption but to also include us forever in the fellowship of His family.

Father, thank You so much for the gift of Your Holy Spirit and the promise that He will live in me forever! Tune my heart to hear His gentle whisper, and help me center my life around the light of truth and grace His presence brings. In Jesus's name.

WINDS OF CHANGE

*"The wind blows where it wishes
and you hear the sound of it,
but do not know where it comes from
and where it is going; so is everyone
who is born of the Spirit."*

JOHN 3:8 NASB1995

"Whoa, did you feel that?" the young girl gasped and looked up at her mom as they walked toward the car. She slipped her small hand into her mother's, the larger one instinctively closing around it as they both stopped to look around. In the distance, they saw the trees bending and swaying under unseen power, the same strong wind that had almost blown the little girl over.

"Look at that wind," her mom whispered, awestruck.

"But I *can't* see it!" came an almost instant reply, the confusion wrinkling the girl's brow.

"But you can feel it, can't you?" her mom challenged. "And you can see what it's doing to the trees, right?"

A beautiful smile spread across her face like a rainbow. "Yes! And I can hear it too," she beamed in wonder, turning back toward the trees to watch the mystery unfold.

We, too, encounter mystery when we consider the Holy Spirit. We can't see Him with our eyes, but we see His power, genius, and love all throughout creation. Greater still, for those who are in Christ Jesus, we feel Him and can even hear His still small voice of truth flowing through our thoughts like a gentle breeze in the sails of our souls. We can't see the Spirit, but we can watch in wonder as He helps us understand God's Word and apply it to our lives. In following His lead, we end up looking more like Jesus—a sign to others who are watching us that God is real, and His awe-inspiring power is at work in us who believe.

God, Your ways are not my ways nor are Your thoughts like mine. You are mysterious, and yet You have chosen to reveal Yourself through the Word, the works of Your hand, and the wonderful counsel of Your Holy Spirit. God, teach me to stop, look, and listen to Your leading. In Jesus's name.

THE THRONE

*"If you then, being evil, know how
to give good gifts to your children,
how much more will your heavenly Father
give the Holy Spirit to those who ask Him?"*

LUKE 11:13 NASB1995

The mom and dad looked at each other, rolled their eyes, and sighed simultaneously as they joined the end of the long and winding line. Stretching before them and their two very excited kids were dozens of other families waiting for their turn to sit on Santa's red-suited knee and whisper their hearts' wishes just above his curly, white beard. To the parents, it was worth the sacrifice of time and money to see their children's faces light up with the wonder and mystery of it all—even though they knew the paid actor on North Pole's throne was powerless to provide anything more than a moment of fun.

Unfortunately, many people—even Christians—approach God with the same level of expectation as those parents. We'll attend church because it's tradition, and we pray because it's part of the Christian package, but privately we doubt that God really cares or can help with what's on our hearts. And truth be told, sometimes our prayer requests sound a lot like kids before Christmas. But unlike the jolly gift-giver of children's fantasies, our God is real and His Father's heart cares more for us than we could ever dream. He has a treasure trove of blessings stored up for His kids, but not the kind that lines store shelves. Far better, God deeply desires to give us the gift of His Holy Spirit, the One who always delivers the hope and joy every heart longs for.

For the believer, prayer is not a formality; it's free access through Jesus into all the power that heaven holds and is foundational for cultivating closeness with God. Our Father, seated on His eternal throne, is thrilled to hear us ask for His Spirit. It is the very gift He is most eager to give us every time we ask for more.

Father, I believe that You have my best interests at heart and that You always deliver what You promise. So I'm asking You today to give me more of Your Holy Spirit so that the desires of my heart will line up with Yours. Thank You for Your generous heart! In Jesus's name.

UNDER THE HOOD

And the Holy Spirit helps us in our weakness. For example, we don't know what God wants us to pray for. But the Holy Spirit prays for us with groanings that cannot be expressed in words. And the Father who knows all hearts knows what the Spirit is saying, for the Spirit pleads for us believers in harmony with God's own will.

ROMANS 8:26-27 NLT

*H*ey, can you hand me my wrench and those clamps on the shelf?" her husband called from underneath the hood of their broken-down car.

Curious, she bent down alongside him to see what might be the matter. Under the hood, though, she was lost. She couldn't tell a serpentine belt from an oil stick, and the maze of tubes and screws and parts she couldn't even identify overwhelmed her. "I don't know how you know what you're doing," she marveled, wondering how anyone ever invented engines in the first place. As far as cars were concerned, she only appreciated that they worked—she didn't worry about how.

"I'm glad you're here." She patted her husband's back and left him to his magic as she patiently waited back in the driver's seat. A few minutes later, the car was ready to roll.

In many ways, our lives are like that car. We operate our days at full throttle, rarely giving thought to what makes us run the way we do or why. But our soul's Designer is intimately acquainted with all our ways and knows our thoughts even before we think them. Like the wife, we might not understand all the ins and outs of what God is doing and why, especially during difficult trials, but we can trust Him to take care of us and restore us every time we give Him access to our brokenness. God's Spirit is an ever-present help in times of trouble, and a faithful Friend. When we lack wisdom, strength, provision, comfort, or counsel, He is only a prayer away, eager to help fine-tune and fuel our faith in Jesus and steer us in the direction of God's heart.

Father, thank You for sending a Helper who understands me even better than I understand myself. Thank You for being an ever-present help in every situation I encounter. Teach me to trust You more as You work in my life, even through the breakdowns, so I can know You more. In Jesus's name.

ONE AND ONLY

I keep asking that the God of our Lord Jesus Christ,
the glorious Father, may give you
the Spirit of wisdom and revelation,
so that you may know Him better.

EPHESIANS 1:17 NIV

*H*er alarm pierced the morning silence. She looked at the clock; it took a few minutes to get her bearings. *What is today?* she wondered in a haze until her memory awakened and she smiled. *Ah, it's Wednesday—the day to have lunch with my grandparents.*

Defying the odds, both of her grandparents were in their nineties and were still sharp as a nail. After sixty-five years of marriage, their love for each other seemed sweeter and stronger than ever. In conversation, each helped the other tell their stories seamlessly, as if the years had solidified their minds and memories into one. It was a pleasure to witness their unity and love, and to hear their lively stories expressed through their different personalities. She couldn't help but think that relationally they had struck gold—that precious balance of uniting with another while retaining individuality.

Relationships like this elderly couple enjoyed are rare, but they reveal a tiny glimpse of the beauty of our great, triune God. Make no mistake; our God is One, as He reminds us throughout His Word. But He also elaborates on the mystery of His nature: He is three in persons. God the Father and Jesus the Son and the Holy Spirit are the same in substance yet distinct in roles and expression. They have lived in loving communion from eternity past and now invite us into that incredible fellowship through faith in Christ. In Jesus, we are known by God and fully loved, and His indwelling Spirit links our hearts to His with a power and permanence unlike any other relationship on earth.

Father, thank You for sending Your Son Jesus to pay the debt for my sins on the cross. Thank You also for sending Your Spirit to live inside me, guiding me ever closer to Your heart. I love being in Your family! In Jesus's name.

WINNING
THE LOTTERY

Now to each one the manifestation
of the Spirit is given for the common good.
I CORINTHIANS 12:7 NIV

*J*erry Selbee loved patterns. He had looked for them in every corner of the world around him for as long as he could remember. But after he and his wife, Marge, retired and sold their convenience store in Evart, Michigan, Jerry discovered a pattern of numbers that paid incredible dividends. Using a legal loophole in the state's Winfall lottery system, Jerry realized that if he invested enough in tickets during the roll-down phase of the game, he would win more than he spent—*every time*. In nine years, he won 27 million dollars. More remarkable than the experience of winning the lottery every month was the way Jerry and his wife chose to spend it. Instead of keeping it all for themselves, they invested most of their prize money in their small hometown. In time, the worn-down, impoverished place took on new life, and business owners and homeowners alike began thriving with the unexpected economic boost.

As believers, we're winners of much more than a monthly lottery defined by worldly dollars. Every day, God has gifted us with all the riches of heaven since we are coheirs with Jesus. Empowered by the Holy Spirit, we have everything that we need to live godly, productive, and purpose-filled lives. In fact, God has even prepared the good works that He wants us to do. But God hasn't poured out His Spirit on us and in us for us to keep Him to ourselves. In the overflow of God's abundant grace and mercy, we bear the fruit of His goodness in order to build up His people and bring the lost into His light.

Ask the Lord to lead you to the people He wants you to encourage today. Offer others the hope, forgiveness, patience, and love that God has richly lavished on you. Let the rebuilding begin.

Father, Your extravagant grace makes my life rich. You are my portion, my daily bread, and the source of all that is good in my life. I want others to see and experience Your goodness too. Please use me to build up the body of Christ and bring others into Your light. In Jesus's name.

MIND GAMES

For the desires of the flesh are against the Spirit,
and the desires of the Spirit are against the flesh,
for these are opposed to each other, to keep
you from doing the things you want to do.
GALATIANS 5:17 ESV

Instead of hitting the snooze button, she rolled out of bed and reached for the leggings and T-shirt she had set out the night before. *Today is going to be different,* she assured herself. She mentally rallied her body as she tied her sneakers and headed for the car. With water bottle in hand, she walked with confidence into the gym, determined to turn over the leaf of laziness she had settled into during the cold winter months. But as she sat down at the overhead press and put the pin into the stack of weights beside her, she hesitated. *This is hard,* her mind argued against the resolution to pursue health. *It probably won't make much of a difference anyway. Wouldn't you rather go sit in the massage chair?*

The longer she sat, the louder the clamor in her mind became, all the while keeping her completely immobilized on the weight machine. Finally, she fought past the fog of doubt and discouragement and started the reps, pressing through the pain, and eventually found her rhythm.

Changing our minds and our behaviors takes time and true effort; it's a battle against the old ways to establish a new and better routine. The same dynamic holds true in the spiritual realm. God's Spirit gives His people the desire to live like Jesus, but we still have our old habits that can sabotage the Spirit's call if left unchecked. It's a daily mind battle to quiet the worldly clamor and cling to God's ways instead. But through prayer, patient persistence, and faithful obedience, we will see our fleshly desires shrink and our reliance on the Spirit strengthen. God is building the power of His love into our lives. We can trust Him.

Lord, the Spirit is willing, but my flesh is so weak. Help me to desire the way of life that You want for me. Help me to fight the sinful part of me that gets stuck in the old unhealthy ways of thinking and renew my mind with Your truth so that I will stay the course and grow strong in Your Spirit. In Jesus's name.

CENTERED

"It is the Spirit who gives life; the flesh is no help at all. The words that I have spoken to you are spirit and life."

JOHN 6:63 ESV

*D*espite the nervous onlooking crowd, the man appeared calm and controlled as he grasped the long balancing pole in his fists. Then he took a step out onto the tightrope that stretched out before him, linking the two high-rise buildings together in an unnatural connection. Those watching collectively held their breath as step-by-step he walked away from the rooftop's safety and onto the precariously thin line of support, the only part of the material world separating him from the certain death that awaited should he fall. It was a balancing act like no other, with his entire life literally on the line. The farther toward the center he went, the more the wire swayed. But the pole in his hands balanced his slow and steady movement forward, keeping him centered and confident. Finally, after ten-minutes of agony that felt like a lifetime, the daredevil reached the opposite building and waved to the cheering crowd, his signal of success.

While we may not understand what possesses people like the tightrope walker to step out with such audacious faith, as Christians we can relate to a certain degree. When we give our lives to Jesus, we begin a walk of faith that progressively leads us away from what feels safe and normal in the world and into an adventure of trust in Jesus. It can feel isolating and lonely at times, when others who are watching think we've lost our mind, and they beckon us to come back to their perceived safety. Pressure from the culture around us swirls like harmful winds, threatening to throw us off our tightrope of faith. But supported by the Spirit and gripping tightly to the Word of God, we stay confidently balanced by truth and grace. By persevering step-by-step, our eyes focused toward Jesus, we will reap the rewards God promises to those who faithfully finish the race.

How are you doing in your faith walk today? Are you still on the edge, afraid to move forward? Or are you trusting the Holy Spirit and the Word of God to direct your steps? Don't be afraid. Unlike the tightrope walker, God's grace surrounds you like a harness, tethering you to His love. Even if you stumble, you won't fall headlong, because your Father is holding you all the way.

Father, thank You for giving me Your Holy Spirit and the Bible, my helpers to keep me centered in the truth. Teach me how to let go of what's comfortable and learn to trust Your lead through this life until I reach the safety of heaven's shore with You. In Jesus's name.

FAKING IT

"Yet a time is coming and has now come when the true worshipers will worship the Father in the Spirit and in truth, for they are the kind of worshipers the Father seeks."

JOHN 4:23 NIV

*T*he front door banged open as the teenager slung her backpack to the floor and made a beeline for the kitchen. Eight hours of intense schoolwork had taken its toll, and now she was starving. She searched the pantry and fridge, finding nothing that satisfied her craving. Then she spied a new basket of fruit that she assumed her mom must have purchased for just such an occasion. She grabbed the apple off the top and took a big bite. Immediately, she spat it out. "Ugh! What is this?" she frowned as she examined the fruit that now exposed the Styrofoam underneath its wax coating. Then reality dawned: it was only decoration. Frustrated by the deception, she threw it away and resumed her search for something real.

Unfortunately, many people who have sampled the Christian life in churches that initially looked inviting have felt a similar sting. Pastors and other church members may appear genuine at first, but after certain pressing circumstances, their inner mettle gets exposed because the shiny exterior doesn't hold up to what's inside. Sadly, hypocrisy in the church has turned many away from the faith.

But Jesus desires truth in our innermost being, and He calls each of His children to live lives of full authenticity. We may be tempted to "fake it 'til we make it," but God's way of trust and dependence is better. Instead of faking the fruit that isn't in our lives, we can simply and humbly come to God for help. Sit at His feet and soak in His Word. Listen for the still small voice of the Spirit, and ask God to search us for anything in us that offends Him. As we repent and turn to Him, gratitude for the gift of grace starts to grow, along with our awareness of how desperately we need Him every moment. As we learn to cling to the Vine as our only source of strength, we will bear the kind of fruit that brings glory to His name and helps others find Him too.

Father, I don't want to be fake. I want to know You and worship You in spirit and in truth, which requires me to be honest and for You to help me see where I've bitten into lies. Grow me up in the truth by changing me by Your Spirit from the inside out. In Jesus's name.

PRUNING PROGRESS

*No discipline seems pleasant at the time,
but painful. Later on, however, it produces
a harvest of righteousness and peace for
those who have been trained by it.*

HEBREWS 12:11 NIV

It had been weeks since she first poked the avocado seed with toothpicks and balanced it carefully on the rim of the water glass so that the seed half rested in the liquid. Slowly, she saw roots begin to shoot down into the water and a single green seedling emerge from the top. Over the next several weeks, the stem grew stronger and taller, sprouting sizable green leaves. "Now we're getting somewhere," she muttered to herself as she consulted the website that had provided all the proper care instructions for her plant project.

"Uh-oh," she sighed as she continued to read. Apparently, when the plant stretched to eight inches tall and sprouted leaves, she was supposed to cut it back down to a short stem. "I don't want to cut off the leaves," she argued with the directions. "What if I end up killing it?" Yet she followed the instructions, trusting the source of the information. Just like the webpage predicted, over the next month the seedling grew back—only this time stronger and thicker than before, yielding more leaves than it did at first.

God, who created plants, has designed the same pruning process to work with His people too. As the Master Gardener of our souls, He desires to see us grow up strong in the faith and be fully prepared to yield healthy and lasting fruit. But strength comes through the cutbacks. Every time we endure difficulty and trials in our lives with an attitude of full surrender and trust in the Gardener, we grow stronger. Suffering is certainly not fun, but the problems we encounter in life are not simply obstacles to avoid or overcome. Often, right in the middle of our confusion and sadness, our Savior is waiting to show us firsthand His sufficiency in our situation and our lives. As we learn to draw nourishment from His Spirit alone, our faith springs up; in turn, we are able to encourage others to trust in God as they endure similar hardships. In this way, we all grow stronger together in the Lord and bear sweeter fruit for Him.

Lord, I don't want to run from You in times of trial. Teach me to trust Your process of pruning out the sin and strengthening me by the power of Your Spirit to produce real fruit in Your time. In Jesus's name.

DYING DEVOTION

*"Greater love has no one than this,
that someone lay down his life for his friends."*

JOHN 15:13 ESV

In 2007, scientists discovered a lone *Graneledone boreopacifica*, a deep-sea octopus searching the depths of Monterey Bay, California, for a place to lay her eggs. For months, then years, the team returned to track her progress. Their findings dumbfounded them all. Laying a comparably small number of tear-shaped eggs cemented to a rocky wall, the mother spread her tentacles around her clutch and began holding tightly. She continuously directed fresh currents to gently wash over them, bringing them needed oxygen for growth, while protecting them from predators with her own body. With pure devotion, the mother never left her post for fifty-three months, the longest brooding period ever recorded in history. But the commitment came with a cost: her own health and strength. In the provision, she gave her own life so that her young would grow strong and live.

As human parents, we can relate to the deep-sea octopus's dedication to her offspring. But even the depths of our commitment and concern for our

children pales in comparison to God's heart for His family. Leaving the glory and comfort of heaven, Jesus came to earth and lived with perfect righteousness— all so that He could lay His life down for us. Jesus showed us what love looks like as He stayed on the cross until death, taking the punishment for our sin on Himself. The payment for the debt of our sin now satisfied through Christ's sacrifice, God raised Him up to become the Savior of all who put their trust in Him. Everyone who seeks shelter under the outstretched arms of God will find comfort and security in Jesus.

Do you ever wonder if God really loves you? Let your doubts die at the foot of the cross. If Jesus went to such great lengths to save us while we were still sinners, surely He stands guard over us now, seeking to strengthen and sustain us as His treasured children.

Jesus, without You, I wouldn't know what love is. Thank You for Your life of faith and perfect obedience to the Father, paving the way so that I could grow and live. Help me to live for You today. In Jesus's name.

STATIC NOISE

If I speak in the tongues of men or of
angels, but do not have love, I am only a
resounding gong or a clanging cymbal.
I CORINTHIANS 13:1 NIV

*H*er road trip to the beach was on point. Sun streamed through the windows, warming her arms and legs as she drove the back roads of farms and fields, winding her way to the beautiful Gulf Coast. Making the most of her time, she turned on some tunes from a nearby radio station as she cruised along.

Slowly, though, the signal began to lose its strength. The static noise that simmered behind the songs soon began screeching louder than the music itself. Though she strained to hear the melody, not wanting to lose the connection, she saw that her persistence was getting her nowhere. The signal was lost, and silence over static became the better choice.

In a similar way, Scripture tells us that our lives send out a signal to those who are around us. With God's Spirit inside us, our life has the power to ring with the sound of God's mercy and grace. We can live out God's message of love when we stay grounded and connected internally to the "signal source." But if we drift too far away from the Father, distracted by worldly worries or drawn to old habits, we will inhibit the outflow of His Spirit. If our lives aren't rooted in the love of Christ and nourishing others with the fruit His presence yields, then our lives will emit a chaotic static that signals to others to tune us out. Without love, we lose our purpose and the power Jesus intends for us to use to build His kingdom.

Do you have people in your life that you find difficult to love? Do you feel like you've lost your signal strength by not staying close to the Savior? Jesus invites us all to return to Him in repentance and humility. He will strengthen and establish you so that your heart sings His praise and your love shows up loud and clear to the world around you.

Lord, I'm lost without Your love. I need You to change me and mold me into Your image so that I can love other people the way You do, from the heart. Please give me a heart like Yours so that the world will see You in me. In Jesus's name.

NEW LIFE

"I am the vine; you are the branches.
If you remain in Me and I in you,
you will bear much fruit;
apart from Me you can do nothing."
JOHN 15:5 NIV

*H*is son was frustrated. For weeks he had waited to see the tender shoots spring up from the soil that he had prepared in a cup and carefully placed in the windowsill where it could soak up the sun's rays. Finally, he asked his father for help. "What am I doing wrong?" he groaned, handing his dad the Styrofoam cup. "It's got the dirt and the sun, and I've watered it every few days," he explained, completely befuddled.

"Well, Son, did you put the seed in there?" the dad queried, quietly trying to cover all the bases. The son's face instantly fell as he realized his failure. In his distraction with all the preparation, he'd forgotten something essential. The soil was empty of what was required for any potential growth! No matter how hard he worked, without a seed, his plans were bound to fail.

Just as there is an order to events in the physical world, the same holds true for the spiritual realm. In order to have growth, first there has to be new life,

even if it's as small as a seed! God tells us in His Word that we must first be born again before we can love like Jesus. We must first come to Him in repentance for our sins and place our faith and hope in Jesus as our Savior. When we do this, He places the seed of His Spirit right into the soil of our hearts. Then, over time as we soak in the warmth of His Word and water our souls through time spent in prayer and fellowship with Him and the family of God, we get to witness the miracle of real growth. Over time, as we yield to God's pruning and nourishing, our lives begin to unfold foliage, then flowers, then the fruit of His indwelling presence. In short, we start to truly love others and live more like Jesus.

If you are frustrated today with your attitudes or actions, check with Jesus, the Master Gardener. Ask Him to put His seed of Life in you. Then rest under His care and allow the promises of His Word to strengthen your faith.

Jesus, I need You. Thank You for dying on the cross to pay for my sins so that I can belong in Your family forever. You have birthed new life in me by the power of Your Spirit. Please grow me up in my faith so that I may represent You well. In Jesus's name.

SOUL FOOD

When they had finished eating,
Jesus said to Simon Peter, "Simon son of John,
do you love Me more than these?"
"Yes, Lord," he said, "You know that I love You."
Jesus said, "Feed My lambs."

JOHN 21:15 NIV

*W*henever he put on the chef suit his wife bought him years ago for Christmas, the whole family knew what lay in store for them. Their dad loved to cook! He'd pore through recipe books to find just the right meal for the occasion. Then he'd go to several stores in search of every ingredient needed for the experience. Finally, he'd set up stations in the kitchen to cover every course his meal required. Then when the food was fully prepared, he called the family to the table.

As much as he enjoyed the preparation, he was most pleased when they tasted the fruit of all his effort. Seeing the delighted smiles and hearing their applause and satisfied approval sent his spirit soaring. Through serving them good food, he showed them his love, and his family happily received them both.

This earthly father is not alone in getting such joy out of loving and serving his family. Our heavenly Father feels the same way! As the source of all love,

He longs to lavish His goodness on our lives in every way imaginable. But it doesn't stop with us. God gives us the richest of fare from His table so that we can share the experience with others.

What does it look like to feed God's people? We can literally invite them into our homes to share our table and lives. We can sit with the babies during church so young families can listen to the sermon together. We can teach our own kids about the goodness of God as we go about our daily routines. Like the chef, we prepare to love by first spending time with our Savior (the secret ingredient for all nourishment and success). Then, we seek opportunities to share publicly what we have learned in the privacy of our time spent with Him. In feeding others with His love, we'll draw others back to the bounty of God's goodness again and again.

Jesus, I love You. I want to show You that I mean it through the way that I love and serve Your people. Please open my eyes to the needs around me and use the time, talent, and treasure You've given me to spread a feast of Your love out for others to enjoy. In Jesus's name.

PEEKABOO
(I SEE YOU)

Hagar used another name to refer to the LORD,
who had spoken to her. She said, "You are
the God who sees me." She also said, "Have
I truly seen the One who sees me?"

GENESIS 16:13 NLT

They were supposed to be watching the preacher at the pulpit. And to be fair, they were listening. But someone a lot smaller was stealing the show. A young toddler with curly blond hair and brilliant blue eyes stood backward in the pew, clinging to her mother's shoulder and staring at the family behind them. Utterly distracted, the dad in the row behind caved to the cuteness and began covering his face with the bulletin, then quickly but quietly moving it away, whispering the words, "Peekaboo! I see you!"

The toddler's eyes instantly sparkled as a huge grin spread across her little face. She began to giggle as the dad repeated the hide-and-surprise game several more times. Surveying the sea of stoic faces around her, the thrill of being suddenly seen by someone never seemed to wane. She laughed all the louder with each successive sighting, as the whole family facing her enjoyed her delight.

Sometimes wide-eyed, wonder-filled children

can preach more truth to our souls than sermons from the pulpit. Their faces clearly tell what their hearts feel without fear of what others will think. It's not surprising, then, that Jesus commands us to come to Him with eyes and hearts as wide open as these little ones. But it's not a silly game with God. He wants us to see Him and know that He sees us—not through eyes of judgment or disappointment, for the cross took care of that. His gaze on us burns brightly with a love and affection so intense that our hearts can hardly conceive it. We are not lost in a sea of billions of other people on this planet. He has singled out each one of His children to give us His attention and show how deeply He delights in us. When we realize He's watching us, the whole world opens up to us in wonder.

Today, keep your eyes open to where God will surprise you with His smile, His blessing, and His joyful, attentive presence in the midst of your ordinary routine. Then reach out to those around you who need to know He cares and sees them too.

Father, thank You for seeing me and loving me the way that You do. Help me to trust in Your love so that I can help others see how delightful it is to focus on You. In Jesus's name.

DEEP LOVE

Above all, keep loving one another earnestly,
since love covers a multitude of sins.

I PETER 4:8 ESV

*A*s she walked down the steep stone path toward the dock, light glistened on the still smooth surface of Smith Lake. Only a few early-rising fishermen in their boats rustled the calm waters in the cool of the morning. Finally at the shore, she surveyed the vast expanse before her, marveling over the mirrored reflection of the tree line and blue sky overhead. *Does it get any better than this?* she thought as she stepped onto the dock and sank down into the Adirondack chair that beckoned her to stay and savor the beauty.

But what her eyes couldn't see lay nestled some 264 feet below the languid surface. In 1961, the Alabama Power Company purchased that valley and the river that ran through it. Lining the river was the small town of Falls City, Alabama. The power company purchased the land (along with every building and car) so they could dam up the river. They wanted to cover *everything* with the deepest lake waters, creating a whole new world above for water lovers to enjoy. Beauty buried the old life of Falls City.

Believer, we get to witness the same miraculous wonder every day of our lives in Jesus. By His power, He purchased our pardon on the cross, paid for with His perfect blood. Jesus, the Living Water, has been poured out over our every imperfection. His beautiful love covers the multitude of offenses from our past, present, and future. We are forgiven and set free to soak in the light and beauty of His love. But that's not all.

He calls us to join Him in the covering. We reflect the beauty of what He has done for us every time we overlook the offenses others do to us. The power of pure love is profound: it changes the landscape of our souls so that we only see others through the lens of God's love. It's a supernatural transformation that happens as we daily submit to His Spirit inside us. Today, ask the Father to help you let go of any old grievances or roots of bitterness that may be building in you. Cover over them with the love of Christ so that the world around you witnesses only His beauty.

Jesus, thank You so much for covering over all of my sins at the cross. Because of Your great mercy, I have been made completely new. Strengthen me by Your Spirit today so that I can reflect the beauty of Your love and forgiveness to everyone around me. In Jesus's name.

THE PAINTING

And now these three remain:
faith, hope and love.
But the greatest of these is love.
I CORINTHIANS 13:13 NIV

*H*e couldn't have guessed how powerful a painting could be until he encountered Rembrandt's masterpiece housed at the Hermitage Museum in St. Petersburg, Russia. Utterly riveted by the emotional drama depicted in *The Return of the Prodigal*, he felt himself drawn into that moment the bedraggled son returned from his rebellious life of debauchery and now bowed at the father's feet, seeking forgiveness. Standing close by was the older brother, frustrated by the lavish, unmerited favor and love the father's embrace clearly showed. The portrait of the father's pure love juxtaposed against the older brother's brooding judgment couldn't have been captured any clearer: mercy triumphs over judgment.

In I Corinthians 13, we encounter God's portrait of love painted with words through the Apostle Paul. Consequently, it has become a favorite passage to read at weddings as a picture of what true love looks and feels like. Love is not an elusive, ethereal, or unattainable idea. Love is a Person—the God whose

very nature is what our hearts cry out to receive. First Corinthians 13 helps capture what love is and what it is not, but description is only the painting. A mere reflection. The real power of love rests in Christ alone, a power and capacity we receive when we accept the love of God into our hearts through faith in Jesus. Like the father in Rembrandt's painting, our heavenly Father enfolds us in His embrace and clothes us with the royal robes of His righteousness. He welcomes us into the feast of His love, and He extends the invitation outward to others.

Without the God of love ruling in our hearts, we have no power to love others. If we try in our own efforts, our lives only look like the elder son who stood aloof, misunderstanding the father's grace. Beloved, Jesus calls us to run into His embrace. Receive His unmerited favor and feast with the Father. As we enjoy His bountiful blessings, our lives will overflow to others with all the goodness of God.

Father, I feel Your arms around me, Your love lifting all the burdens from my weary heart. Flood my soul with Your saving grace. Fill me with supernatural love, joy, and peace. Use this broken vessel to pour out Your love to everyone around me. In Jesus's name.

STAYING POWER

Jesus knew that the hour had come for Him to leave this world and go to the Father. Having loved His own who were in the world, He loved them to the end.

JOHN 13:1 NIV

*T*he elderly man gently eased his wife of forty years out of bed and onto the chair beside the vanity. Instinctively, he began brushing her long gray hair and talking over her shoulder, telling her about the upcoming day's events. He knew she wouldn't remember the details; many days she didn't even remember who he was. Alzheimer's had stolen her memory but not her husband's devotion. Day in and day out, he ensured that she stayed safe and comfortable, though she couldn't comprehend the level of commitment her care required. He would walk her through her last days until she went home to heaven, no matter the personal cost.

In a day and age where our culture quickly cancels whoever and whatever stops working for them, we seldom see the kind of commitment that keeps on going, especially in the face of difficulty. Worldly love ebbs and flows with the tides of emotion that drive it, leaving people longing for something that will last.

Jesus shows us what real love looks like. Not only

did He go to His death determined to free us from our sins, but He also rose again to the ultimate place of power where He persistently prays to the Father on our behalf. Best of all, He promises to never leave our side. Like the woman with Alzheimer's, we're quick to forget His goodness and are apt to wander away from Him. But by the power of His indwelling Spirit, He keeps us close, guarding our hearts and minds until we reach heaven to be with Him forever.

God's love doesn't come and go like the version of love we often see in the tumultuous relationships around us. God's love stays and affords us the stability we need to learn, grow, and love even the unlovely around us with a persistence that won't quit.

Today, are you feeling fatigued from that family member, neighbor, or coworker who takes more than they give or seems incapable of being kind? Ask God, the source of true love, who never gives up on you, to give you extra grace. Pray for the people who are challenging to love. And ask God to supernaturally love them by the Holy Spirit's power.

Lord, You have certainly loved me through all of my messes, and You've never quit on me. Thank You for Your rich mercy. Please empower me to love like You, committed to the people You place in my path, until You call us home. In Jesus's name.

BOUND TO LAST

Even more than all this, clothe yourself in love.
Love is what holds you all together in perfect unity.

COLOSSIANS 3:14 NCV

"Mom, what are we going to do with all these shells?" the wide-eyed, sand-covered seven-year-old wondered aloud to her mom as she carried the overflowing pail back to their spot on the beach. In an effort to encourage the search, her mom had pointed out which kinds were keepers and which ones were better left on the shore. Now joining their loot together, they toted a large haul of colorful treasures from the sea.

"After we rinse off the sand and dry them, we're going to make a big picture frame with them!" her mom declared, deciding on the fly.

But the astute little girl frowned with concern. "But the shells have so many different shapes and sizes. Some of them are broken and have sharp edges. How are we ever going to get them to stick together?"

The mom smiled. "I've never seen a project that a little hot glue can't fix."

All seasoned crafters know this mom is spot-on. When you use the right binding agent, even the most

unlikely objects can and will stay right where you place them.

Even if you're not the crafty sort, God still has a similar secret that will help us mend and maintain the relationships in our lives. No matter how different (and sometimes unpleasant) the people who He places in our path may be, He provides the most powerful bonding agent in the universe to unite us: His unchanging love. Like shells on the seashore, people's personalities and souls liven up the world with God's creativity and color. Instead of complaining about our differences, we honor and delight God when we perceive their value and appreciate their beauty simply because each unique person is an image-bearer of God. Rich or poor, educated or simple, seasoned believers or new to the faith, we all fit perfectly into God's family as His Spirit glues us all together in the love of Jesus forever.

Lord, You've outlined many different ways that we can honor You, but they all have one common bond: love. It's Your love that holds us together. So please pour out Your kind of love through me so that my relationships are blessed with permanent peace. In Jesus's name.

LAY IT DOWN

For what is our hope or joy or crown of boasting
before our Lord Jesus at his coming?
Is it not you? For you are our glory and joy.

I THESSALONIANS 2:19-20 ESV

*I*t wasn't that Jonathan didn't understand what was at stake. As the king's son, he stood to take over the throne when his father, King Saul, stepped down. So when David stormed onto the scene with a major score over Goliath and the Philistines, Jonathan should have felt threatened. He could have plotted David's undoing like his dad did.

Yet Jonathan didn't join in his father's jealous scheming. Instead, he recognized God's sovereign hand working out a divine plan that he didn't dare try to circumvent or foil. He committed himself to God and devoted himself to David with a love that looked otherworldly. Loyal to the very end, Jonathan laid down every right and claim to the crown and covenanted to defend and protect David until his dying breath.

In the same way, God calls His kids to come out from the surrounding culture of self-focus and selfish ambition. He calms the frenzied clamor to compete with everyone else and offers a radically different way to live and love. Like Jonathan, we can seek to build

others up—even when doing so would seem to set us back. We can nurture, pray for, protect, and promote others to rise higher, even as we kneel lower before the foot of the cross. Jonathan shows us what John the Baptist also recognized: God must increase as we decrease. The way of God's love is to lay down our own lives so that God's glory rises and the watching world will be drawn to Him.

Today, if you feel the weight of comparison and competition crushing your spirit, simply repent and remember who determines your worth. Relinquish every hint of selfish ambition and rest in God's sovereign plan for your life. With self-preservation out of the way, we shine the light of God's love for others with a brilliance that brings hope to our broken world.

Lord, so much of my stress comes from my fear of failing or falling behind everyone else. I confess that in those times, I'm simply not trusting You to take care of me and direct me. Forgive me, and train my mind and heart to think and love like You. In Jesus's name.

PRACTICING HIS PRESENCE

You make known to me the path of life; in your presence there is fullness of joy; at your right hand are pleasures forevermore.

PSALM 16:11 ESV

*A*s soon as the car pulled into the drive, the old woman watching through the window smiled. The van's side doors slid open, and out poured all three grandchildren. The aged woman came out to meet them, receiving her toddling grandkids in her open arms. After giving her grown daughter a hug as well, they all went inside where the two youngest boys took immediately to the new Tonka trucks their Mimi had bought for just such an occasion. The granddaughter sat by the toybox and sifted through the stuffed animals to find her play partner for the day. Seeing her kids were contented and quiet, the daughter turned to her mom. "So, Mimi," the daughter began, "what's on the agenda for today?"

Mimi shrugged her shoulders and smiled again. "My agenda is simply being here with you all. It doesn't matter what we do or where we go, as long as we're together."

Spending time with the people we love most feels like a slice of heaven. Even if it's just sitting in a room together without a word spoken, the connection heals our hearts and soothes our souls like no outing or accomplishment ever could.

Imagine seeing our connection to the Savior in this same light! Throughout Scripture, Jesus beckons us to believe in Him and His love for us—a love that has the power to dispel every fear. In His presence, the Bible says we find the very fullness of joy—full like the feeling after the finest meal. Who wouldn't want to fill up on loads of joy?

But like all real relationships, cultivating closeness takes time. Could you use more joy, more healing, more peace in your life? Do you long to feel loved no matter where you go or what you do? Then start your day by getting away from all the busyness life demands. Draw close to Jesus by sitting in a still, quiet place where you can tune your attention to the Spirit's gentle voice, spoken through the pages of Scripture. Let Him stir your heart to deeper devotion. When we savor Jesus's presence and sit still long enough to line our hearts up with His, we witness the wonder of a joy-filled life, no matter what kind of circumstances come our way. Today, draw near to your God, and He promises to draw near to you, bringing heaven's joy with Him.

Jesus, nothing in this world compares to the joy of spending time in Your presence. Please help me eliminate the distractions that keep me from coming to You on a daily basis. Fill me up with the joy of Your Spirit. In Jesus's name.

RESTORING HOPE

This day is holy to our Lord. Do not grieve,
for the joy of the Lord is your strength.
NEHEMIAH 8:10 NIV

When they began the project, the house looked like a total loss. Rotting wood lined the doorways and window sashes; parts of the ceiling dangled down from above; and random trash left by the previous owners littered the stained and torn carpet below. But the house flippers didn't mind. They were in the renovation business! The team split up to tackle different problem areas based on their expertise. As they continued to put their skills and sweat to work, a beautiful transformation began to unfold. The formerly dilapidated structure became sound and secure and aesthetically pleasing—a desirable place for any new family to inhabit.

What made the renovation team work so hard, day after day? They didn't get bogged down by the disaster in front of them because they knew what it would look like in the end. Their vision for the house's potential and the prospect of a future payoff propelled them to persevere.

As believers, we can look at our broken-down, fallen world in much the same way as that worn-out house. We can concede that our culture is crumbling and the prognosis is grim unless intervention happens. But we are in God's restoration business! We have the power of His Spirit inside us to heal what's broken and bring hope to the hurting. Even in the middle of the day's difficulty, we don't despair. The joy of God's Spirit fills us with strength as we stick to His restoration process, one person at a time.

When you turn on the news or scroll through your social media feeds, do you feel like all is lost? Look up to the One with the master plan that promises eternal redemption. Let the joy of His indwelling Spirit fill you with energy and strength, knowing that God certainly finishes every work He starts. Remind yourself that earthly efforts for His kingdom promise eternal rewards that far outweigh your current struggle. Today, thank God for the opportunity to join Him in His kingdom work and fill you with joyful hope as you work together to restore beauty.

Father, I praise Your name because You are good and You restore what's broken. Thank You that I can experience Your joy to the full even while I'm working through dark and difficult trials, because I know You make everything beautiful in its time. In Jesus's name.

ABRASIVE BEAUTY

*Consider it pure joy, my brothers and sisters, whenever
you face trials of many kinds, because you know
that the testing of your faith produces perseverance.
Let perseverance finish its work so that you may
be mature and complete, not lacking anything.*

JAMES 1:2-4 NIV

A crowd of onlookers on the pier watched the scuba diver disappear below the surface of the bay waters. Within just a few minutes, he reemerged with a handful of oysters plucked from the sandy bottom down below. Everyone gathered around as the partner on deck took the oysters and began opening them one by one. Some contained only the creature inside. But others bore a beautiful white pearl, sitting as if on a pillow for presentation. "Ooooh," the crowd reacted in approval, applauding the great reveal as the shucker slid the pearl into the box beside him for safekeeping.

Then he turned to the people. "This beauty actually comes from irritation," he began. "A little food particle or bacteria slips inside the shell and lodges into its mantle, the muscular wall protecting the mollusk's organs. In self-defense, it secretes a protein and mineral-based liquid that coats the intruder, rendering it harmless," he explained. "Over time, this process produces the beautiful mother of pearl we all appreciate today." Everyone applauded.

When we wear pearl necklaces or earrings, hardly anyone thinks of the long and difficult process that shaped the iridescent treasures. The same is true for trials and difficulties we encounter in life. The Bible says that when we encounter hard times, we can receive them with joy. As abrasive and intrusive as the circumstance may seem, God will use it to cultivate the kind of character inside of us that He desires. Patience and perseverance yield a heart of praise and thanksgiving when throughout the difficulty, we trust that God is up to something good even though we can't see it yet. His refining process always takes time, but the resulting treasure is always worth the wait.

What struggle or trial are you currently facing? If you belong to Jesus, there's no need to fret or even force the difficulty away. Instead, look up to your Father whose Spirit supplies you with the joy and trust you need to coat the difficulty with His care. Rest in His process, and it will yield a life of remarkable beauty that brings wonder and joy to the watching world around you.

Lord, please help me to trust You when I encounter trials of many kinds. It's trusting Your goodness that brings me true joy regardless of my circumstances. I believe that You are working out everything for my good, and I'm grateful for the process. In Jesus's name.

SIGHT AND SOUND

Therefore if you have any encouragement from being united with Christ, if any comfort from His love, if any common sharing in the Spirit, if any tenderness and compassion, then make my joy complete by being like-minded, having the same love, being one in spirit and of one mind.

PHILIPPIANS 2:1-2 NIV

When she purchased the tickets for her video-game-loving family, she couldn't have guessed how great the experience would actually be. She just knew an orchestra was coming to town, playing all the musical scores from their favorite Zelda games. When the day finally came, the family filed into their seats along with other gamer fans and waited for the show to start.

Suddenly, large screens behind the orchestra lit up with familiar scenes from the game's fantasy worlds. Simultaneously, flutes and oboes, drums and cellos joined in unison with all the other instruments, overwhelming the audience with the wonder of full orchestral sound. Coupled with the background visuals, the epic sounds sent the audience into another world of adventure and mystery, valor and purpose. Even those who never played the video game at last understood why the game had garnered such respect and enthusiasm from young and old alike. Sight and sound united as a powerful portal into a life grander than their own.

In a similar way, God unites His people to produce a powerful, epic effect on the world around us. Though we each have distinct personalities and unique gifts, God's most powerful expression of love unleashes when we unite them to build His kingdom. In the marriage of sight and sound—visually, demonstrably living out our faith while verbally telling others about the goodness of God—people will finally begin to understand what the buzz of the gospel is all about. In uniting and working together, God's people also encounter a surprising and otherworldly experience: real joy. Together we are overwhelmed with the wonder of God's kingdom purpose, which is far bigger and better than anything we could conceive or achieve by ourselves.

Father, I want to experience the joy of working together with Your people to tell others the epic story of Your great love expressed through Jesus. Help me to humbly accept my role in the greater scheme of what You have planned so that others will see and experience Your glory. In Jesus's name.

ON REPLAY

Rejoice in the Lord always;
again I will say, rejoice.
PHILIPPIANS 4:4 ESV

*L*ast year was a rough season. Granted, the football teams they had played against were 6A, with some of their guys twice the size as the players Coach had to work with on his team. But the seasoned coach knew their success moving forward depended on how well they learned from their past failures and triumphs. So he holed himself up in his office and ran the tapes from last year's season again…and again… and again, until he gained a greater understanding of how to lead his team. In replaying the old scenes, he began to see new patterns that paved the way for a more promising future season.

In our hurried culture today, we rarely take time to reflect on the past. We tend to press forward to the next day, the next goal, and the next event and end up running lives full throttle without real direction or purpose behind the relentless pursuit. Too often, people come to the end of their time here on earth regretting what they did or didn't do.

Like the football coach, we won't make that mistake if we adopt a replay strategy. Scripture encourages us to consider the past, not only of our own lives but also of the history of mankind as recorded in God's Word. Look back all the way to the very beginning of time to see God's intent and purpose for putting His people on this planet. Consider the joy and success God's people saw every time they placed their trust in His care. In contrast, reflect on the devastating results of rebellion against His ways. Like the coach, if we carefully study the way God's purpose and plan played out in the past, we can know which way is best to pattern our lives now.

Do you feel like your life is pushing ahead at warp speed without a good reason why? Take time today to stop and reflect on who God is and what matters to Him—that you matter to Him. Remember the joy that comes from walking in step with His Spirit and that leaves an eternal legacy. Then hit replay again each day, pausing to reflect, remember, and ultimately rejoice in God's great love for us, and that in Him, we always win.

Father, thank You for the continual invitation to remember Your goodness, Your faithfulness, and Your purpose for my life. Help me to stay rooted in truth and rejoice always because You are my God. In Jesus's name.

CROWNING ACHIEVEMENT

"Nevertheless, do not rejoice in this, that the spirits are subject to you, but rejoice that your names are recorded in heaven."

LUKE 10:20 NASB

*I*t was Honors Day, and all the parents sat quietly in the back of the auditorium, straining to see where their son or daughter sat in the section of reserved seats in front. Palpable excitement filled the air in anticipation of the announcements to come. Then a man clad in cap and gown with golden cords and tassels dangling down each side of his robe strode across the stage to take the microphone. He welcomed the guests, explained the proceedings, and emphasized the importance and value of each award he held in his hands. "Will my child win?" each parent wondered.

But once the ceremony concluded, the buzz settled down. Back at home, the certificates were stuffed into baby books or tacked onto walls as paper memories of profound moments that, while showing potential, still lacked any power to actually secure their future success.

The disciples experienced a similar situation when Jesus sent them out on their first mission assignment.

Afterward, they returned to home base, super-stoked by all the supernatural miracles they saw unfold as they healed the sick and exorcised demons. Truly, it was impressive work. But Jesus responded with a profoundly different perspective: "Do not rejoice that the spirits are subject to you..." The disciples were excited by what they could now accomplish, but they missed what mattered much more. "Rejoice that your names are recorded in heaven," Jesus reminded them.

As people who chronically try to prove our own worth by what we do, we need to intentionally remember what actually matters. The root of real joy lies in recognizing and reveling in what Christ already accomplished for us through the cross. Spirit-led activity for the kingdom comes from first understanding our identity in Him. The apostle Paul later even adds that our earthly achievements are worthless trash compared to knowing Christ. God alone is worthy of glory, and our connection to Him is our source of everlasting joy.

Lord, I don't know why I get caught up in pursuing worldly success when You are really who I need for life. Realign my heart with Yours. I rejoice today because I belong to You! In Jesus's name.

MORNING SONG

The whole earth is filled with awe at Your
wonders; where morning dawns, where
evening fades, You call forth songs of joy.
PSALM 65:8 NIV

*I*t was still dark when she got up, tense about all that would unfold that day. "So much to do, so little time," she whispered in the dark as she donned her robe and headed for the coffeepot, her first pit stop for the day. Out of the corner of her eye, she caught sight of the rising sun.

She opened the back door for a front-row view. Hues of rose, then gold gilded the wispy clouds now visible against a pale blue sky. Like a conductor, the light cued life all around her, the rising song of several birds ignited the morning with the sound of... "Joy?" She mused as she listened to the chorus of all different kinds of birds breaking the morning silence with their own songs of praise. Like the dawning sun, a realization of God's sovereignty washed over her, warming her heart and soul. "God is in control," she worshipped out loud, her heart now joining in song with the birds. Suddenly, her to-do list seemed less pressing as she rested in the reality that God cared for her far more than the beautiful world all around her. Wrapped in the comfort of His love, she got ready for work, no longer frazzled by demands but now focused on the One whose sovereign hand would see her through this day.

With the frenetic pace many of us keep, life can feel more like a chore to endure than an experience to enjoy. Remembering Jesus, however, can change everything. The psalmist reminds us, "This is the day the Lord has made!" Our God has crafted this day, this moment, with all the intentionality He wielded when He first created the world. He has packed each day with purpose—for you to know Him and make Him known. Rejoice in His presence, and remember that He stays with you everywhere you go. The watching world will wonder about your source of joy, and you can lead them to Jesus!

Father, thank You for giving me another day of life and another chance to declare Your praises. In Your presence, my joy is full and fuels me to live my life in the worship and wonder of who You are. In Jesus's name.

THE FORECAST

The hope of the righteous brings joy,
but the expectation of the wicked will perish.

PROVERBS 10:28 ESV

For years, she had dreamed of her wedding day. As a nature enthusiast, she pictured a lovely outdoor setting in mid-spring when the gorgeous Sakura trees circling her favorite lake bloomed. In her mind's eye, she could see herself in beautiful white, her veil flowing as she descended down the garden path between a small gathering of friends and family who watched as she joined her betrothed who waited with the pastor under a canopy of cascading pink flowers.

And now, her dreams were about to come true. She had found the one her soul loved, and they had made plans for the perfect day to wed. Except... now that the day was upon them, the forecast disagreed. Storms threatened to steal the moment, filling her with stress and sadness. Frustrated, she felt that all was lost. So her mom drew her close and redirected her thinking. "It's not the location that brings the beauty," her mom encouraged, "but the beginning of two lives becoming one, no matter what the weatherman predicts or the clouds produce."

We all can relate to this bride. We want our lives—

like a wedding—to be picture-perfect. But instead, we often find ourselves experiencing heartache and difficulties we never dreamed we'd face. Like the bride, our disappointment can lead to despair if we don't call to mind a greater reality: God's prospect for our future is planned, perfect, and permanent with Him. We will one day shed this sin-stained, pain-filled world and will link hands and hearts with Jesus when we meet Him face-to-face in heaven. No matter what we're facing here on this earth, the forecast for God's people is fullness of joy. Our perfect day awaits us when we will take our permanent place in His arms to be loved and cherished forever. Today, celebrate the joy of your holy union with the God who loves you now and forever.

Lord Jesus, You did tell us that in this world, we will have trouble. But I can take heart because You have overcome the darkness. I long for the day when my eyes will see you face-to-face, but until then, I'll keep my hope and heart set on You. In Jesus's name.

LOVE LANGUAGE

Our mouths were filled with laughter, our tongues with songs of joy. Then it was said among the nations, "The Lord has done great things for them."

PSALM 126:2 NIV

She was so giddy she couldn't hide it. One of her roommates instantly noticed the moment she walked through the door and plopped down opposite her on the sofa. She was beaming.

"Sooo, how was your date?" she giggled in anticipation of a great story. A huge smile spread across the girl's face as she threw her head back, thinking of the best way to convey what she had just experienced.

"He. Is. Amazing." The emotions of the night flushed her cheeks with a rosy glow. As she recounted each gentlemanly gesture and their genuine and deep conversation, her eyes sparkled with unbridled joy. Never had she felt so seen and known by someone else. Never had hope for the future shined so brightly. Her world had changed through an encounter with love, and unmistakable joy like rays from the sun emanated from her in every direction.

"Wow! I'm jealous!" her roommate laughed. "I want to meet the man of my dreams too!"

The look of love is unmistakable. Whether it's shown from lover to lover, parent to child, or friend to friend, the deep devotion and commitment comes out in our words, our laughter, and the entire way we live. Real love and joy are always linked because they both come from the same source: Jesus. When His Spirit reigns inside of us, we experience a closeness to our Creator that no other relationship on earth can rival. In the depths of our soul, we are fully seen, completely known, and utterly loved.

As we encounter Jesus and spend meaningful time with Him each day, gratitude and joy surge within our souls, spilling out in words and actions that shout to the world just how great God is. When others witness the undeniable joy we've found in our relationship with Jesus, they will want to experience Him too!

Lord, truly in Your Presence there is fullness of joy. There is no other God like You! You are my hope and shield, my fountain of life and joy. Please let others hear of Your goodness through my words and actions today! In Jesus's name.

NEW LIFE

"I tell you that in the same way there will be more rejoicing in heaven over one sinner who repents than over ninety-nine righteous persons who do not need to repent."

LUKE 15:7 NIV

In a flurry of activity, they loaded the suitcases they had already prepared, and alerted their family. By the time they reached the hospital, so had her sister and parents. Everyone was wide awake and eagerly awaiting the moment of new birth. But all the planning in the world could not have prepared the new parents for the flood of joy and awe they both felt when the doctor held up their newborn son and placed him in his mother's arms. Soon, the father stepped outside the room and announced the birth of a healthy baby boy. Shouts of joy and squeals of delight rang out from the waiting room, everyone thrilled about the arrival and miracle of new life.

Babies bring us so much joy because their very lives are precious and packed with future potential. They are entering into life's adventure on this earth, and we have the opportunity to pour love and hope into them as they grow.

Angels can relate! God gives us a glimpse into heaven's waiting room filled with angels eagerly anticipating the next soul to be saved. Every time a person on earth repents of their sins and surrenders to Jesus as their Savior, a new creation is born and all of heaven rejoices in the miracle. The old is gone, and the new work of grace has begun! This precious soul is now packed with all the power and potential that comes when the Spirit breathes new life into their spiritual lungs. We, too, celebrate here on earth with joy whenever we witness someone being born again into God's kingdom. Every soul saved becomes a new member of God's family, our new brother or sister in Christ.

Lord, what a miracle new life is! Thank You for each person You place in my path. I want to see them born into Your kingdom through the power of Your Spirit. Please teach me how to lead them to You as You work the miracle of new birth in them. In Jesus's name.

THE SEARCH

"Peace I leave with you; My peace I give you.
I do not give to you as the world gives.
Do not let your hearts be troubled
and do not be afraid."

JOHN 14:27 NIV

The past few years, she could feel it creeping in. First, she felt it in her fingers that ached whenever she tried to open jars. Then it surfaced in her toes as she walked her usual route around the neighborhood. But when her knees, wrists, and ankles revolted against her will to work out, she sat down at her computer and began searching for a solution. Instantly, she found scores of medicines, herbal remedies, and suspicious life hacks that all promised relief from her encroaching arthritis.

But she was skeptical. Some of the claims seemed too good to be true. So she read the reviews, only to realize that those, too, were sponsored ads. What at first looked like promising endorsements turned out to be manipulative attempts to elicit her purchase. "I just want something that actually works, in real life!" she moaned as she closed her browser and headed off to bed, her shopping cart still empty. *Tomorrow,* she thought, *my search will continue.*

Unfortunately, most people spend their whole

lives searching for a solution to the persistent problems they experience in life. Lies from the culture abound, promising that if we have enough power, or money, or success, then surely we will be able to sleep better at night and attain that ever-elusive peace our anxiety-ridden souls so desperately crave.

Jesus understood the search. He'd seen people scrambling for solutions and quick fixes ever since sin wrecked perfection in the Garden of Eden and racked our lives with fear. But Jesus knew the only solution people really needed: Himself. He is our shield and deliverer. He is our hope. And He is our firm foundation in an uncertain world. When we are feeling stressed out and overwhelmed, His Spirit nudges us back into His waiting arms where comfort in His sovereignty and care abounds.

Lord, thank You for giving me the kind of peace that prevails over every situation I encounter. Your peace is real and lasting because Your love and presence in my life never fails. I gladly leave my worries in Your hands and rest in You. In Jesus's name.

THE KEY TO PEACE

Do not worry about anything, but pray and ask God for everything you need, always giving thanks. And God's peace, which is so great we cannot understand it, will keep your hearts and minds in Christ Jesus.

PHILIPPIANS 4:6-7 NCV

"Oh no!" she said out loud as she sat in the driver's seat, empty-handed. Without her keys, she was stranded in her own driveway, along with the kids who carpooled with her to school. Instinctively, she pulled out her purse and dug through the contents, carefully searching for her keys in every corner. But with each passing minute, her panic only increased.

Agitated by stress and her surging blood pressure, she exited the car and tore through the house, checking every normal nook and cranny where she could have possibly placed them. "Vanished! They have just completely disappeared!" she concluded, exasperated by the interruption to their morning routine.

"What's that in your back pocket?" came the question from behind her as her son peeked his head in the door to help her search. In disbelief, she reached around and felt the familiar key ring shape poking out of her pocket. With a sigh of relief and a word of thanks for the help, she headed back to the car to continue on her day.

Just like the mom, we often panic when we aren't prepared for life's curveballs—particularly the painful kind. We get all wound up trying to find the solution to our pressing problems so that we can work our way out of it. And when we can't, we're quick to despair. But God reminds us that we have the key to lasting peace in our "back pocket." Freedom begins the moment we remember that God has gifted us with the power to pray right in the middle of our most stressful, difficult moments. God promises that He not only hears us, but He will work everything out in our favor as we trust Him. When we release our fears and concerns before His throne, He floods our hearts with a deep peace that leads to praise.

Lord, prayer is powerful because You are a God who cares and acts on my behalf. Please forgive me for forgetting to call on You throughout my day. Please strengthen my prayers and fill me with Your divine peace. In Jesus's name.

THE PATH

Therefore, since we have been made right in God's
sight by faith, we have peace with God because
of what Jesus Christ our Lord has done for us.

ROMANS 5:1 NLT

When they signed up for the mission trip, they understood the risks. Riding across a war-ravaged country where national laws meant very little, the team of medical missionaries relied on their guides to get them to their destination. But as darkness fell, a shadowy figure walked out onto the dirt road, blocking their way and brandishing a machine gun.

In the middle of what seemed to be nowhere and with no route of escape, the vulnerable team grew tense. But the Sudanese pastor leading the charge appeared unfazed. He simply exited the car and approached the soldier, speaking in his native language. Documents and payment were exchanged, and he returned to the car with a smile on his face. "Carry on!" he called out to the driver as if nothing had happened. The team, though, knew their friend had saved their lives and removed the obstacle to their destination.

Even if we never go to a third-world country, we all live in a world ravaged by sin. We live and work in a spiritual war zone, with evil forces all around determined to steal, kill, and destroy our lives (John 10:10). But those who travel through life with Jesus as their protector and guide never need to fear. He has gone before us and knows the terrain. He has negotiated with God to pay the price required for our safe passage from this life to our final destination of heaven with Him. Though unexpected twists and turns happen in our lives along the way, Jesus comforts us with the irrevocable truth of His perfect provision. We have peace with God that lasts forever. What can mere man do to us?

Today, reflect on the price Jesus paid to secure your permanent position in God's family. No power in the universe can ever separate you from His infinite love. His life has bought us perfect peace forever.

Lord, I admit that life can be frightening at times, especially since I don't know what the future holds. But You do, and You are my God, my Guide, and my forever Friend. Thank You for making a way for me to be with You always. In Jesus's name.

OVERCOMERS

"I have told you these things,
so that in Me you may have peace.
In this world you will have trouble.
But take heart! I have overcome the world."

JOHN 16:33 NIV

The young gymnast approached the beam with determination. With every twist, leap, and flip, she steadied herself, willing her body to stand solid and straight, centered on the beam. But the difficult back handspring, backflip combination caused her to lose balance. After battling the air, wildly shifting her weight, and waving her arms to regain her position, she simply couldn't recover and fell to the mat below. Shaking off the defeat, she remounted the beam and finished her routine. She felt frustrated, but her coach smiled at her, knowing a secret: she was the only gymnast in her age bracket at the competition! No matter how she performed or what score she achieved, she would receive first place medals!

It wasn't her performance that earned the medal; it was her position in the category. The same is true for those of us who are in Christ Jesus. His love and provision at the cross puts us into a different category than everyone else in the world who doesn't know

Him. Others are competing and fighting their way through life to prove their worth. But we get to rest in God's favor that we've already won in Jesus. We may falter at times in our faith and succumb to old patterns of sin, but like the gymnast, we can "remount the beam" by confessing our sin and returning to Jesus. No matter what the world throws at us or how badly we wobble, our victory in the end is secured by our position in Christ.

Today, don't let the weight of past or potential future failures worry you. Set your focus on Jesus as you steady yourself in the truth of your immovable position in God's family. Jesus reminds us that in this world we will have trouble. But we can take heart! He has overcome the world!

Lord Jesus, I praise Your name because You have defeated sin and death at the cross. Thank You for Your great mercy and grace that helps me get up when I fall and centers my hope back on You. Because of Your victory, I win in the end too. In Jesus's name.

CONNECTING PEACE

They must turn from evil and do good;
they must seek peace and pursue it.

I PETER 3:11 NIV

*F*irst, he sorted all one thousand puzzle pieces, carefully putting all the flat-edged pieces in one place and the rest in categories according to their colors. Then carefully, one by one, he inspected each edge until he found the connecting link. Slowly, a line of connection began to form, bending upward and back around when corner pieces were added until a giant rectangle formed on his kitchen table. "Now the real fun begins," he alerted his wife who took notice of his progress whenever she passed through the room.

Hours turned into days of tedious searching, finding, and placing each piece where it belonged. Slowly, the same picture from the box began to surface on the tabletop...all the way until the very end when, to his horror, he noticed a piece—the last piece—was missing! The fun activity turned into an all-out hunt under the table, in the trash, and everywhere else until at last, it was found stuck to the inside edge of the box.

Some people stay away from puzzles because it's

just too difficult or demanding to find the way all those different pieces fit together. Unfortunately, sometimes we have the same mentality toward people, steering clear of their sharp edges, which can hurt or annoy us. But God desires for us to come together in Jesus! Our unity reveals His glory—the great picture of Jesus that forms when we love and serve one another.

So how do we, as the body of Christ, navigate all the different personalities and opinions of people God cares about? The Bible says we must seek peace and pursue it. Literally, go after it until you find it! Look for ways to eliminate division and discord. Look for ways to bring connection to your situation in any way you can. In this way, we're following Jesus's master picture of life and are far more likely to link others to Him.

Jesus, sometimes I just react to situations instead of looking for ways to help calm the chaos and create unity. Settle my soul by the power of Your Spirit and help me be a link of connection with Your peace. In Jesus's name.

SWEET DREAMS

In peace I will lie down and sleep,
for You alone, Lᴏʀᴅ, make me dwell in safety.

PSALM 4:8 NIV

She knew it was going to be a long night. It was only early afternoon, and already the neighborhood kids had started shooting off their fireworks to celebrate Independence Day. "But it's not too fun for you, is it?" she tried to soothe her labradoodle, who stood at the window watching the activities and barking in displeasure.

As the night wore on, the claps and explosions only grew louder and more frequent. Tense with fear, the dog's whole body trembled as he cowered under the table for cover, certain that something awful was happening outside. So she coaxed him into her own bed for the night, covering her frightened companion under her blankets and arms. Soon, his breathing slowed, and deep, restful sleep ensued.

So what made the difference? The fireworks didn't diminish, but the comfort of his owner's covering calmed his anxious heart. The truth is, God's presence meets us in the same way! So often we lose sleep over a host of worries that explode in our minds even through the wee hours of the night. We allow fear to rob us of the joy and peace that could be ours if only we understood the situation differently. Just like the dog, we have a Master who loves us more than we can even imagine. He cares about what concerns us, and He doesn't want us to cower in fear or fret throughout our days and nights. Instead, He welcomes us to take refuge in His powerful and capable arms. He covers us completely with His perfect love. God's goodness enables us to lie down each night in rest and live each day in peace.

Today when you are tempted to worry, or if you're tossing and turning at night, remember Whose you are. Take hold of the truth that God is holding you, the shield of His love completely surrounding you. And rest, knowing you are covered in His care.

Jesus, how sweet it is to know that whether I am awake or asleep, You are with me and taking care of me. Teach me what it means to cast my cares on You, and deepen my trust so that I can stay settled in the peace Your presence brings. In Jesus's name.

THE WHOLE WAY

You, Lord, give true peace
to those who depend on You,
because they trust You.

ISAIAH 26:3 NCV

Brenda Spahn and her daughter, Melinda MeGahee, had a radical idea: "What if instead of just releasing prison inmates back into the world where they failed the first time, we help rehabilitate them until they make a full recovery?"

Working together, they began inviting recently released women into their own home, helping them get back on their feet. As they saw more and more success, the need grew greater than their home could contain. So, Brenda and Melinda prayed.

God provided every penny necessary to secure an old hospital building and renovate it to become what Brenda dubbed a "whole way house." "Whole," she smiled, "because God doesn't do anything halfway!" Today, thousands of women and their children find wholeness together through the ministry services the Lovelady Center provides.

When we hear stories like Brenda and Melinda's, we marvel at the magnitude of their faith's impact. But God has packed the same potential into each person; that potential comes to fruition when we apply the same truth that propelled the Lovelady leaders to step out in faith. Real trust in Jesus reveals itself in declared and dedicated dependence on Him. As we focus our faith and fully hope on the person of Jesus and trust Him to direct our steps in the way we should go, we discover a whole new world of peace and purpose. Problems become opportunities to turn once again to the only One who knows the right solution. And our weakness opens the door for our Savior to demonstrate His strength.

Do you long for peace and fulfillment each day? Direct your thoughts and prayers toward God and hold fast your focus. Tune your ears to His Spirit and turn your feet in whatever direction He is leading you, not in halfway trust but in wholehearted devotion. Then watch in awe and wonder as His peace steadies you through the adventure of following Him and producing fruit of eternal value.

Lord, today I fully fix my eyes and mind on You.
I believe that You have works prepared for me to
do today. I will not worry about the how, because
I know Who will be my help. In Jesus's name.

PRACTICE MAKES PEACE

*Whatever you have learned or received or heard
from me, or seen in me—put it into practice.
And the God of peace will be with you.*

PHILIPPIANS 4:9 NIV

He was waist-deep in the Gulf Coast waters, enjoying the powerful waves that roared around him. Fish darted at his feet, and the sun warmed his shoulders while he worked his way across the shallow sandbar. But suddenly, his feet slipped off the edge, and he sank down into the deep chasm between the banks. Instantly, a powerful rip current pulled him under and away from shore.

Panicking, he fought to return to shore, kicking and paddling hard against the current. But after a few minutes of futile effort, he remembered what his swim instructor taught him years ago about riptides. In his mind's eye, he even saw the chart that showed the only way to exit a current of this kind. Though it railed against his instinct to fight, he submitted to what his instructor had said. Suddenly he began swimming parallel to the beach instead of toward it, gaining more ground than he had before. After a few more strokes, he swam safely out of the current, floating on his back toward sandy refuge.

When we encounter difficult dilemmas physically, emotionally, or relationally, our instinctive "fight or flight" kicks in. Panic and stress can send our blood pressure soaring, hearts pounding, and minds racing with all the "what ifs" our imagination can conjure. But God calls us to calm our harried hearts and remember in those dark times what He taught us in the light.

His ways may seem counterintuitive, but our Creator knows what we actually need. When we stop flailing in self-effort and start following what He told us to do, we begin to gain spiritual ground. Suddenly, the reality of His powerful presence sinks in, securing our souls, and guiding us back to where His peace prevails.

Today, don't let stress or panic pull you under. Instead, put God's Word into practice and let His peace wash over you in the divine process.

Father, I don't know why I let my mind run amok with all the what ifs, when You are the One directing my life. Today, I choose to hand over my fears to You and trust You to take care of me. In Jesus's name.

MENDING THE MESS

If people's thinking is controlled
by the sinful self, there is death.
But if their thinking is controlled by the Spirit,
there is life and peace.

ROMANS 8:6 NCV

*T*he young seamstress seemed flustered. Finally, she threw up her hands in frustration and motioned for the instructor to come and help. "Just look at what keeps happening." Her agitation was obvious as she held up the mangled cloth for examination. "No matter what speed I keep the pedal, it just ends up all bunched together and matted in these ridiculous knots."

The instructor inspected the mess. "Let me see what you're doing with another, fresh piece," she calmly requested. So the girl tried again, this time under her mentor's watchful eye. "Oh yes, I see the problem," the instructor observed. "You're forcing the fabric through instead of letting the machine do the work. You need to relax your grip and simply let it slide under the needle," she advised. This time the student let the pedal and needle work its magic as she watched her fabric pull straight. "Now you're on track!" her teacher smiled.

Sometimes life can feel like that tangled,

mangled fabric. No matter how hard we try, we can't straighten out the people and situations that are robbing us of peace and sleep. Nothing we say or do seems to have any effect on their course of action, which leaves us feeling hopelessly frustrated.

But God gives us insight in Scripture that sets us free. Instead of trying to control others and force our frustrating situations in a direction that feels more pleasing to us, God invites us to surrender to His ways. Invite His Spirit into whatever situation you're facing, and let God direct the flow of your relationships and life. As you release your grip of control and learn to rely on His Spirit to lead the way, you'll experience His joy and peace. Just watch as He mends the pieces of your life together in better and more lasting ways than forcing it in your flesh ever could.

Lord, whenever I take matters into my own hands, I get frustrated and mess things up even more. Please forgive me! Help me to rely on Your Holy Spirit in patient and persistent prayer as I wait for You to direct the course of my life. In Jesus's name.

IN EVERY WAY

Now may the Lord of peace Himself give you
His peace at all times and in every situation.
The Lord be with you all.

II THESSALONIANS 3:16 NLT

*H*e had plotted and planned for her birthday, pulling out all the stops. So when she followed him into the restaurant expecting dinner for two, her jaw dropped at the scores of family and friends shouting, "Surprise!" She loved the conversations and stories shared, memories from a lifetime collectively relived with laughter and joy.

But the night wasn't over. Having arranged for them to go to their grandparents', he brought his wife home to a trail of rose petals leading to the bathroom. There she discovered a warm bath drawn, scented soap flowers floating on the water, and lit candles with more flowers lining the bathtub rim. "All this is for me?" She turned toward her husband, who hoped she was happy with all his efforts.

"Yes, I just wanted you to relax and feel fully immersed in my love for you," he replied with a smile he couldn't contain.

"I do!" she radiated back as she slipped under the fragrant warm water and felt the weight of the world slip away into peace.

Because of our broken world, we all work very hard to secure whatever it is we think we need to feel loved and at peace. Whether it's fun, food, a hot-stone massage, or a weeklong trip to the Bahamas, we're willing to spend whatever it takes to earn a moment of blissful rest and relaxation.

But Jesus surprises us with a gift that goes far beyond what money can buy or others can give. He has pulled out all the stops to show us how much He loves and cares for us in every possible way. As we begin to see and understand the reality of His love, we slip into the warmth of His all-encompassing peace that washes over our minds and souls. We no longer live in fear, frantically pursuing temporary pleasures. We are permanently inundated with the perfect and prevailing peace of His presence, protection, and provision. In Him, we find soul rest that lasts forever.

Jesus, surely You have blessed me in every way, surrounding me with Your love and filling me with Your peace. Help me to live each moment of my day fully aware of Your presence and provision for me. In Jesus's name.

ABOUT TIME

*The Lord is not slow in keeping His promise,
as some understand slowness. Instead, He is
patient with you, not wanting anyone to perish,
but everyone to come to repentance.*

II PETER 3:9 NIV

She looked at her watch for the third time in the same minute as she paced back and forth on the front porch. "Where are they?" she worried out loud, wondering where the movers were whom she had hired to bring her belongings to the new house. She calculated the distance from the storage unit to her house and couldn't find any logical explanation for why they still weren't there. She was paying them by the hour, a concerning fact that fueled her imagination with all the ways they could be delayed. Maybe they decided to stop for lunch. Or perhaps got lost? Or wrecked?

At last they rounded the corner and pulled up to the house. Making a beeline toward the driver, she all but yelled, "What took you so long? Didn't you leave three hours ago?"

"Yes, ma'am, we did," the driver confirmed. "But we had to first pack everything up. Then we travel slowly so that bumps on the road don't cause cracks or breaks in any of your fragile belongings," he explained. "Wouldn't you rather us arrive with everything safely intact?" In the end, she realized he was right; his reasoning was more reasonable than her hurry.

In a similar way, it's easy to wonder what on earth God is doing as we watch the world tailspin in pain, confusion, and corruption. *When is God ever going to do something?* we think as we watch disasters unfold on the nightly news. Worse, we begin to lose hope. We grow complacent in our faith, forgetting that Jesus promised to come back for us.

But God hasn't forgotten to come. He's not even delaying. Instead, Scripture says He's simply being patient, waiting for everyone who will repent and receive salvation to do so before judgment day arrives. We join Him in the wait, patiently preparing for the day we're promised to meet Him face-to-face.

Father, Your timing is always perfect, and You fulfill every single promise You make. Thank You for patiently waiting for more people to turn to You and be saved. Help me get ready for Your imminent return! In Jesus's name.

HEALTHY PORTIONS

I say to myself, "The LORD is my portion;
therefore I will wait for Him."
LAMENTATIONS 3:24 NIV

The two men stood side by side, surveying the vast expanse of land stretched out before them in all directions. Clearly, the portion of land watered by the large, winding river looked superior to the rest of the landscape. The lush vegetation and a bustling city lured Lot's attention. "I'll go there," he decided, looking up at Abraham to see if he'd agree.

He did. By all appearances, Abraham had just lost his chance to claim the best land for his family and servants. Allowing Lot to choose first, he was relegated to whatever was left. While his nephew was delighted with the opportunity for the upper hand, Abraham seemed completely satisfied.

What was his secret? He had his sights set on something even greater: God Himself. His lack of selfish ambition signaled to God another display of true trust in God's provision. "Do not fear," God reassured Abraham. "I am your shield and your very great reward." By waiting patiently for God, Abraham gained God's promised protection, provision, and permanent friendship.

Seeking to serve oneself like Lot did isn't just ancient history, though. It's a sin that still permeates our culture, and if we're not careful, it can poison us too. Not wanting to be outdone by others, we compete and work hard to secure the best of everything for ourselves and our family, so that we can enjoy the good life. But God challenges us to let go of our perceived rights and the pursuit of worldly goods. In place of the best possessions and position, He promises to be all that we actually need. Abraham's secret strength was truly knowing God. He hadn't lost out. He'd won first prize!

Today, take note of the times you feel overlooked, lagging behind, or worried about the future. Like Abraham, look up to the Lord whose powerful presence stands right beside you, and wait patiently for Him. He will strengthen your heart and establish you for life.

Lord, You are the strength of my heart and my portion forever. I never want to run ahead of You or seek to forge my own way. I will wait patiently for Your direction, because only You satisfy my soul. In Jesus's name.

PRESS ON

*Rejoice in hope, be patient
in tribulation, be constant in prayer.*

ROMANS 12:12 ESV

*A*ll the little girls were giddy with excitement. It was Anna's birthday, and her mom had many activities planned for the party. Before cake and ice cream, they all sat down around the table for craft time, and Mom passed out some special paper and pens to go with it. "Today, we're going to make our own T-shirts!" she announced, pointing to the sample she was already wearing. "Just draw your design on this special paper, and I will iron it right onto the fabric."

After one girl finished her masterpiece, she brought it to the mom. "Is there a sticker or something on the back of the paper?" she wondered out loud as she watched the mom put the shirt and the paper on the ironing board.

As the iron steamed, Anna's mom pressed down hard and explained the process. "I don't know exactly what the paper is made out of, but it's special. When you turn it face down on the fabric and add high heat from the iron, the picture lets go of the paper and sticks to the fabric instead." The mom smiled as she held up the T-shirt with the girl's sunshine drawing pressed on it.

"That's beautiful!" the little artist squealed in delight, and all the other girls agreed.

Beyond birthday crafts, real beauty is often produced through a similar process. Even when we become Christians, we still have our old habits and worldly ways stuck in our thinking. Left to our own devices, we would all miss growing into the unique, Christ-centered creation the Father intends for us to become. But we don't typically just let go of the bad, any more than the picture could be peeled off the paper. Just like it required high heat and pressure to release the masterpiece, so God forges trials that turn up the heat in our souls, separating out the good from what needs to go.

Are you experiencing any difficulties in your day? Instead of complaining or letting them drag you down, ask God to give you the patience you need to endure your trial or challenge well as He cultivates the heart and mind of Christ in you. Blessings flow when we stay surrendered to His Spirit, no matter what circumstances come our way.

Lord, bring on the heat! Please melt away all the wrong thinking and desires that keep me from loving and serving You and others well. Help me to grow into the person of grace who patiently waits for You to complete Your work in me and others. In Jesus's name.

SIMMER ON THIS

Love is patient, love is kind. It does not envy, it does not boast, it is not proud. It does not dishonor others, it is not self-seeking, it is not easily angered, it keeps no record of wrongs.

I CORINTHIANS 13:4-5 NIV

From the second she woke up, she knew it was going to be a long, busy day. But she was prepared! The day before, she had purchased the ingredients to make her favorite version of Crock-Pot curry. Standing at the kitchen counter, she coarsely chopped up chicken thighs, garlic, ginger, and onions and threw them into the pot. Then she poured in a cup of broth and a boatload of Indian spices.

But right then, one of her kids rounded the corner as he was getting ready for school. "Are you making chicken curry?!" his hopeful voice rose along with his eyebrows. "Can I have some now?"

The mom laughed and shook her head. "It would make you sick if you ate it right this second. I just put it in! It takes all day to simmer so that the chicken cooks and the spices blend together better."

Settling for a bowl of cereal instead, he announced, "Well, I'm so excited for dinner tonight!"

Her son became willing to wait once he realized that sampling the food too early would not taste the same or even be safe. As God's kids, we can apply the same life lesson. Like ingredients for a sensationally savory meal, God tells us plainly what needs to go in (or stay out of) the mix if we want our lives to taste like His goodness. But patience is the slow cooker in which all of life's circumstances and our responses to them are given ample time and space to blend. If our hearts stay warm to God's ways, over time our lives become a pleasing aroma that honors God and points the desperately hungry world back to the only source that can satisfy.

God is not in a hurry, and we don't need to be either. When we are patient with ourselves and with others, we create space for forgiveness, love, peace, and a host of other godly qualities to properly develop in our lives. When this happens, we can leave an impact on others that feeds their souls and lasts for eternity.

Lord, I get impatient when I forget that You are the Master Chef. But I relinquish control of my life into Your loving, capable hands. I look forward to tasting and seeing Your goodness as You complete the work You've begun in me. In Jesus's name.

FLOOR SAMPLE

But for that very reason I was shown mercy so that in me, the worst of sinners, Christ Jesus might display His immense patience as an example for those who would believe in Him and receive eternal life.

I TIMOTHY 1:16 NIV

As she stepped into the flooring store, she surveyed the hundreds of samples lining the room. Knowing that the level of activity in her home between the pets and kids demanded the most durable flooring options, she searched for what seemed best for her situation. After a few minutes, though, she realized that all the descriptions by the samples seemed to be the same. They were all stain resistant, all supposedly sturdy and strong. "How can I find out which one works best?" she finally asked the salesclerk, hoping to end her indecision.

"Well, I have this one right here in my home." He tapped a sample to her left. "We have a Great Dane, two labs, and four kids." He smiled and added, "We installed this in our living room seven years ago, and it's still going strong with hardly a scratch on it!" Then he scrolled through the pictures on his phone. "See, here's a picture of it right here. If it's strong enough to handle my crew, it's strong enough for anything!"

Convinced by the picture, she was sold.

In a world where people and products make all kinds of claims to convince us to trust them, we instinctively become cautious. If something seems to be too good to be true, it usually is. So, we rely on other people's verified experiences to evaluate if we should proceed with the transaction.

The Apostle Paul understood the age-old need for assurance, especially when it came to something as important as salvation. He knew we would wonder if God's mercy and grace could handle all of our messy sins and failures. Like the floor salesman, he points to his own life as evidence—with a full history of the worst of all sins, fully forgiven by God. If God can redeem someone as lost and hopeless as me, Paul says, He can and will do the same for every sinner who repents. We can take that truth to the bank.

Jesus, every day I am amazed at Your patience with me. Praise the Lord that Your mercies are new each morning! Let my testimony of Your forgiveness and grace lead others to find their hope in You too. In Jesus's name.

GROWING BABY CHICKS

For this reason, since the day we heard about you, we have not stopped praying for you. We continually ask God to fill you with the knowledge of His will through all the wisdom and understanding that the Spirit gives, so that you may live a life worthy of the Lord and please Him in every way: bearing fruit in every good work, growing in the knowledge of God, being strengthened with all power according to His glorious might so that you may have great endurance and patience, and giving joyful thanks to the Father, who has qualified you to share in the inheritance of His holy people in the kingdom of light.

COLOSSIANS 1:9-12 NIV

*L*ike most kids, she was full of questions—especially now that she was living on the ranch for a summer with her grandparents. Today, it was five in the morning, and Pop was headed to the barn where the brooder warmed his baby chicks. "What are you doing?" she wondered aloud as she watched his every move.

"Tending to the chicks." His simple reply only fueled her curiosity.

"But why do you change their water and food every day?" she asked.

"So that they don't get sick, and they will grow healthy and strong."

On a roll now, she reflected, "But why do you *want* to grow baby chicks?" She followed at his heels as he replaced the tiny birds' bedding and food.

Turning toward her, he explained, "So that these little chicks will one day be healthy chickens who lay big eggs that we can eat for breakfast!" He smiled and tousled her hair. "So let's go have some now!"

The farmer shared his true motives. He wasn't just interested in chicks; he had a bigger purpose in mind that fueled his daily actions. God does the same thing as He steps in to care for us. Daily He feeds us, cleans us, and creates the best environment we need, not only for this day but for His ultimate purpose for our lives: to grow us up in Christ to be reproducers for His kingdom—to know God and help others to know Him too. We work to please Him, live lives worthy of our purpose in Christ, and grow in the knowledge of God and strength of His power SO THAT we will have great endurance and patience—the two characteristics every Christian needs to persevere in the faith until we reach full maturity in Christ.

Lord, thank You for working in me with great patience and intention. Let my life grow strong under Your care so that I, too, may model Your patience and perseverance as I mature in You and mentor others to do the same. In Jesus's name.

THE REUNION

*But we are hoping for something
we do not have yet,
and we are waiting for it patiently.*

ROMANS 8:25 NCV

*I*t seemed like just another ordinary day, cooking breakfast, getting the kids to school, dressing to go to work. It had been hard since her husband left, though she understood his soldier's duties and prayed daily for his safe return. They exchanged letters as often as possible, and occasionally saw each other through Zoom when his platoon enjoyed a momentary pause from their covert missions. Each connection, each visit kept her going through the weeks and months of his absence. She also worked hard to keep their kids engaged with what was happening with their dad, not wanting them to forget how much he loved them and that he was gone fighting against evil so that everyone could experience freedom.

But suddenly the front door flew open, and a man in fatigues walked through. Instantly their eyes met, and she froze for just a second before squealing with delight, throwing her arms around her husband's neck. Their kids came running in to check on the commotion and cried with joy to see their dad had come home.

As the Bride of Christ, we also are waiting for our Husband's return. Before Jesus left this earth to go back to the Father, He encouraged His followers to stay the course. Keep on mission, keep fighting the good fight of the faith day in and day out as they lived out their calling. But as He reminded them, He also encourages us: wait with hope! He is on a mission to prepare a place for us so that once this spiritual battle against evil is finally over, we'll be reunited to live with Him forever.

Jesus's promised return fills us with the hope we need to keep pressing on as we patiently wait for that glorious day. While we get glimpses of Him now through His written Word, there will come a day when we see Him face-to-face. Like the mom with her kids, we need to keep reminding other believers of the blessed hope that awaits us all at Christ's return.

Jesus, it's so hard being away from You. I long for the day when You will come back and make everything right. I praise You because the victory is sure and that day will come. Help me to wait patiently for You as I prepare myself for that wonderful reunion. In Jesus's name.

RENEWED STRENGTH

Even youths shall faint and be weary,
and young men shall fall exhausted;
*but they who wait for the L*ord
shall renew their strength;
they shall mount up with wings like eagles;
they shall run and not be weary;
they shall walk and not faint.

ISAIAH 40:30-32 ESV

"What is this dead thing?" Her husband held up a curious brown ball of dried leaves as they worked to clean out her great-grandparents' garden shed.

"Oooooh, I remember those!" his wife gushed, the memory sparkling in her eyes as she took it from his hand. "We used to play with them as kids. Just watch what happens when you put it in some water." She filled a shallow bowl and put the small tumbleweed in it to soak. "Just give it a little while," she instructed, as they both resumed their work.

Within an hour, an amazing transformation had taken place. "Look at it now!" She motioned to her husband, who stopped what he was doing to take a look. The wadded, brittle, brown ball now sprawled out before them with full, bright green foliage.

"It's alive!" he gasped.

She laughed at his reaction. "That's the mystery of these little guys. Resurrection plants only look withered. The life inside returns with just a little water."

Sometimes we go through seasons when the situations in our lives leave us feeling dry and brittle—physically, emotionally, and even spiritually. Songs that once brought joy now cease to stir our souls. Energy and anticipation that once fueled our endeavors have now been dried up by the heat of our troubles, and try as we might, we simply can't recover them.

But God says to take courage! Wait patiently for the Lord our Savior to send the rain your thirsty soul needs at just the right time. Instead of worrying about your state of affairs or working harder to fix it yourself, rest and wait for God's fountain of Living Water to revive your thirsty soul and color your life with vibrant hope once again.

Lord, I will not rely on my feelings, nor will I faint in despair. I will wait for You to come and restore my soul. My sight and hope are fixed on You, my fountain of life. In Jesus's name.

THE POTTER'S PLAN

Preach the word; be prepared in season and out of season; correct, rebuke and encourage— with great patience and careful instruction.

II TIMOTHY 4:2 NIV

eautifully glazed, hand-wrought pottery lined the shelves behind the instructor as he faced the class where each participant was seated at their own potter's wheel. "Before we begin, I need to explain the properties of clay," he started, urging them to feel the wet, red mound placed beside each wheel. Over the next ten minutes, he described how to throw the clay on the wheel, step on the turning pedal, and begin to shape the ball of clay into a small bowl. Then he threw some clay on his own wheel and within a minute yielded a beautiful work of art.

The process looked and sounded so simple. But once the wheels started spinning, the clay creations wobbled and warped, falling over before the students could barely get started, let alone complete a finished product. "Apply even pressure against the edges and pull upward with your fingers," the instructor coached, trying to help them stay on track. A few got too frustrated and quit, while others kept reworking the clay until it grew supple in their hands. In the end, they all left with their keepsake creation, though none of them compared with what lined the shelves. "If you want to make art like that," he challenged, "you need to come back for more lessons."

When we place our faith in Christ, God instantly makes us new creations. In a flash, God forgives all of our sins and resurrects our spirit so that we become alive with Christ and can hear His voice through the power of His Spirit and the Word. But like the clay, we are still in process. God works in our lives to remove the blemishes and to shape us into beautiful vessels through which He can pour out His love to the world.

If we want to be used by God for His glory, we've got to stay centered on the Potter's wheel until He is finished. Instead of giving up on yourself or others when life gets wobbly or goes awry, press in and pull up toward God, and stay supple in His capable hands. In His time, He transforms ordinary clay into vessels of His glory.

Father, I confess that I often get frustrated in the process instead of trusting that You're at work. Help me to stay patiently surrendered to Your plan for me and encourage others to do the same. In Jesus's name.

WEED PATROL

*Let all bitterness and wrath and anger and clamor
and slander be put away from you, along with all
malice. Be kind to one another, tenderhearted,
forgiving one another, as God in Christ forgave you.*

EPHESIANS 4:31-32 ESV

*I*nstinctively, she placed her hands on her hips and pursed her lips as she surveyed the overgrown yard behind the house they had purchased. Vines climbed up trees and along the fence, choking out the choice plants she preferred to keep. Thistles, dandelions, and a host of other weeds robbed the good grass of any potential to grow. Rocks throughout the yard threatened her mower and her hopes to level out the whole yard.

"This is going to take a lot of work," she acknowledged out loud as her hands reached for the shovel. But after working for a few hours making little to no progress, she realized a greater reality. "This is out of my league!" she moaned with utter fatigue. "I can't do this by myself. I've got to find someone who can help." So she called a few friends, who graciously came to help her clear the clutter. Together, they tackled the yard and helped her create a space that everyone could enjoy.

When we become new creations in Christ, God

immediately adopts us into His family. We are freely forgiven and filled with His Spirit who promises to stay in us forever. But like that backyard, we enter our new lives in Jesus with old baggage. Before living surrendered to Jesus, misperceptions of God grew like vines twisting around our thoughts and behaviors. Bad habits from our old lives still spring up in our thoughts and conversations like intrusive weeds. And unhealed wounds from the past rock the ground of our souls, limiting the growth of the good things God wants to see take root in our lives.

But Jesus doesn't leave us to work our life's landscape alone. He immediately answers our cry for help and delights in taking the lead on our transformation all of our days. When we listen to His Spirit's daily direction, we learn how to let go of deadly bitterness and self-centeredness and implant the beauty of kindness and forgiveness in its place. Keeping close to Jesus and following the direction of His Spirit inside us, we clear more space for His grace to grow. He makes everything beautiful in His time!

Jesus, I want Your kindness and goodness to grow in me every day. Please till the soil of my heart so that we can pull out the weeds and work Your Spirit of grace into a permanent place in my heart. In Jesus's name.

REACHING TO RESTORE

"But love your enemies, and do good, and lend,
expecting nothing in return, and your reward
will be great, and you will be sons of the Most High,
for he is kind to the ungrateful and the evil.
Be merciful, even as your Father is merciful."

LUKE 6:35-36 ESV

When she found him beside the road, he was covered in dirt, his fur matted in knots and crawling with fleas. The poor mutt cowered with tail tucked as she approached and carefully wrapped a towel around his quivering body. He let out a growl and snapped at her in self-defense. But she calmed him with her reassuring words and slow, careful movements. As a seasoned dog rescuer, she knew the long road that lay ahead. But she was prepared to keep him safe and set him on the path of healing and hopefully future adoption.

At home, she washed away the mud and clipped his mangy fur, fluffing him dry and coating him in flea powder. Already he looked like an entirely different dog. But it took weeks of tender and consistent care to conquer his fears and rebuild his trust after so much trauma. When he was well, she alerted the Humane Society that she had a new pup ready for adoption. Within just a few days, they found him a forever family, and she got ready for the next referral.

When we're working with wounded animals, we know to exercise caution. But our concern for their well-being overrides their hostile resistance to our help because we know they have limited understanding and we have the power to do them good.

God wants us to view people through that same lens of compassion—even the people who oppose us or wish us harm. Because we're filled with God's indwelling Spirit, He invites us to reach out in kindness to bring the hope and healing of Jesus to a lost and hurting world. When we obey, we aren't guaranteed a wonderful response. Just like hurting animals lash out in fear, so do people. But God tells us to persist in kindness and pray for their full restoration. In the process, God blesses us with deeper awareness and awe at His incredible kindness toward us.

Father, I am constantly amazed by Your kindness toward me. Fill me with that same kind of persistent compassion toward others, that my attitude and actions might lead them to adoption into Your family. In Jesus's name.

FAMILY MATTERS

*So then, as we have opportunity, let us do
good to everyone, and especially to those
who are of the household of faith.*

GALATIANS 6:10 ESV

*A*s a designer, she knew how to listen well and
work to find floor plans and design schemes
to suit each client's needs. She enjoyed her work
and found it fulfilling to create aesthetically pleasing
places for the families she served.

But when she and her husband bought a new
house for their growing family, her attention to detail
took on a whole new dynamic. Keeping up with
current styles and trends fell secondary to securing
cozy and comfortable living areas that invited
community and conversation. Knowing the needs
and personalities of each of her family members,
she kept them on the forefront of her mind as she
picked out paint colors, indoor and outdoor seating,
and soothing lighting options. When she was finished,
the whole family instantly felt right at home, finding
everything they needed right at their fingertips. Her
efforts transformed the new house into a functional
space of warmth, light, and love.

As Christians, we know that we are called to
reach out to our communities with the hope and

love of Christ. Together, we are on a mission to build Christ's kingdom, and we have endless opportunities for service. But our Savior reminds us that home matters too...our household with family members and our household of faith with fellow believers. If we're not careful, in our zeal to build the kingdom, we can neglect those closest to us.

But it's our faith family who will live with us forever in heaven. And it's our unity and love, Jesus says, that will let the lost know what life in Jesus looks like. If we want to win the world to Jesus, we must start at home, loving our family well at home and at church. Don't let separation or neglect creep in while you're busy with daily life. Instead, ask God to help you show even deeper levels of kindness to those closest to you.

Jesus, please help me to keep my focus on You and follow Your lead. Fill me with ways to show kindness and love to everyone so that the world can see You more clearly. In Jesus's name.

TABLE TALK

Whoever pursues righteousness and kindness
will find life, righteousness, and honor.

PROVERBS 21:21 ESV

The school bell rang, signaling time for lunch. All the students poured out of their classes and headed toward the cafeteria as the sound of excited conversation filled the halls. But for one middle schooler, the sound signaled dread. Every day, after getting his tray of food, he'd search the room for a safe place to sit, a table where the other kids would include him in conversation. But after a few weeks of repeated rejection, he resolved to sit alone, silently playing on his phone to pass the time, resigned to his fate.

But one day, another much more popular student passed by him to sit at the table with all the other athletes and cheerleaders. Just before placing his tray on the table, he paused, eyeing the young kid in the corner. The Spirit inside him stirred as he considered what to do: stay comfortable with his friends or strike up a conversation with someone he didn't know. Against his own comfort and preference, he took his tray to the corner table. "Can I sit here?"

His question caught the young boy off guard. Though it was awkward at first, eventually conversation flowed, creating a new friendship through a small act of surprising kindness.

Because of God's righteous character, His kids have a special calling. Though we all tend to veer toward what is comfortable and fun whenever we consider what to do at work or in our free time, the Holy Spirit often has another agenda for us. If we stay in close connection to His leading, He'll show us the people He's placed in our vicinity that He wants us to bless. Whether it's the Walmart cashier, the people sitting beside us at our child's athletic event, or our neighbor as we go get our mail, God wants us to pursue—literally run after—righteousness and kindness. When we obey, we will watch God grow connections, build character, and bless us with the satisfaction of walking in His ways.

Lord, please open my eyes today to see those around me whom You want to bless. Give me ideas of ways that I can show kindness to others that will point them to Your love. In Jesus's name.

GOLDEN RULERS

*"So whatever you wish that others
would do to you, do also to them,
for this is the Law and the Prophets."*

MATTHEW 7:12 ESV

*H*er daughter was distraught, arms crossed, and starting to cry. As the mom approached the car where she stood outside, she quickly surmised the situation. Inside the car, sat her son at in the front seat, smiling smugly. Fighting the urge to roll her eyes at the familiar scene, she opened the car door so he could hear.

"What's going on here?" She looked at her son while motioning to her daughter.

"Nothing. I just got here first." His triumph directed toward his tearful sister.

"But I called it in the house, and he always does this!" she retaliated, throwing her fists down in consternation.

"Which one of you is thinking about the other?" the mother queried, trying to quell the situation while pointing both of her children away from their self-serving perspectives. Then she worked to maintain equity and peace as she proposed a workable solution.

Unfortunately, it's not just kids who find consideration of others hard to grasp—and live. Grown-ups struggle in the same way as we strategize how to spend our limited time and hard-earned money the way we want whenever we get the chance. But the Spirit of Christ within us calls us to a different perspective. Instead of seeking to please ourselves, He invites us to consider others' needs as more important than our own! Such deference defies our natural inclinations and demands that in every situation where we're tempted toward selfish gain, we must die to ourselves.

Dying to our own selfish desires isn't fun, but it does develop the kind of life character that Christ demonstrates toward us. As we treat others the way we'd like to be treated, it not only frees us from enslavement to self, but the world also sees the supernatural kindness of Christ in our servant's heart.

Today, instead of self-promotion or entitlement, seek to be a blessing to others. Consider Christ's kindness toward you, and allow His Spirit to flow rivers of kindness through your conversation and consideration.

Lord, I confess that I often care more about myself and what I want and need than I do about others. Holy Spirit, change that. Please help me die to selfish desires and show kindness to whomever You place in my path. In Jesus's name.

UNCLOGGING KINDNESS

Be kind and compassionate
to one another, forgiving each other,
just as in Christ God forgave you.
EPHESIANS 4:32 NIV

The day started with her usual morning routine on track: get out of bed, read her Bible, take a shower, and go to work. But as she stood beneath the showerhead soaking in the warmth and thinking about her to-dos for the day, she felt something odd at her feet. She looked down and noticed the water had risen above her ankles. Stooping down for a closer look, she realized it wasn't draining at all.

But it wasn't a mystery. She'd seen clogged drains before. So after drying off and getting dressed, she grabbed a screwdriver and released the drain cover. Not too far down she spied the culprit: a nest of her own hair and other disgusting debris blocking the hole. Holding her breath, she plunged the yellow, plastic plumbing device deeply down into the pipe and pulled up, releasing the nasty mess and clearing the pipe. Now she could get on with her day!

Clogged showers are gross enough, but God says that clogged souls are even worse. It's a condition that doesn't necessarily happen overnight. It builds slowly over time whenever someone wounds or disappoints us, and we don't let it go. Instead of offering grace and forgiveness, we tuck the trauma deep down and, before we know it, we've blocked our capacity to show any love and kindness toward that person. Worse still, we start to see the nastiness seep up into our conscious thoughts and conversation with others. If we don't clear the problem, the rancid condition will ruin our spiritual health and our witness.

This is why Scripture stresses the importance of forgiveness. Like the plastic plumbing tool, God's Spirit helps us not only see the debris in our souls, but He also pulls it out by His mighty power and cleanses us every time we confess our sins and struggle to forgive. When we release our hurt feelings and wounds to His care, the kindness of Christ is freed to flow through our lives once again.

Lord, help me see when bitterness and unforgiveness are building up inside me. Set me free through Your forgiveness, and help me to extend that same grace to others so Your kindness and mercy flow through me. In Jesus's name.

DEEPLY DIVINE ENCOUNTERS

Therefore, as God's chosen people, holy and
dearly loved, clothe yourselves with compassion,
kindness, humility, gentleness and patience.

COLOSSIANS 3:12 NIV

The couple gathered their gear together and boarded the charter boat, headed toward a spot off the coast where a ship had sunk several decades before. Now the location boasted a host of different marine life, including the Mimic octopus that they both hoped to see. As the boat drew close, all the deep-sea divers donned their wetsuits and strapped on air tanks and weights. Once they were all properly prepared, they anchored the boat and plunged into the water, flippers first. Thanks to the gear and their guide, they were able to swim directly to the undersea wreck and enjoy the encounter with all different kinds of sea creatures.

But what if they had decided they didn't need their wetsuit or air tanks? Wouldn't their underwater sea adventure be short-lived at best, or bound for total disaster at worst? They prepared properly for their excursion because they wanted their mission to succeed. The same goes for believers as we live out the adventure of Christ's kingdom mission. Every day, God opens up opportunities for us to encounter all kinds of people—in our own homes, at work, at church, and in our community. Wonderfully divine interactions can and will take place when we're properly clothed with His Spirit.

As we abide in Christ and submit to His Spirit, we can say no to the sinful inclinations of our flesh and choose to strap on the life-giving air of compassion, kindness, humility, gentleness, and patience that come part and parcel with the Spirit's presence. He goes everywhere we do, enabling us to breathe in the love of God that we in turn exhale out through every word we speak and work of kindness we do. By keeping close to Jesus, we will succeed in His mission for each day.

Who will you encounter today? Ask Jesus to help you prepare by getting dressed for success and staying submitted to His Spirit.

Lord, thank You for giving me everything I need for life and righteousness. Empower me by Your Spirit to put off the world's ways and to live a life worthy of You, filled with Your wonderful kindness. In Jesus's name.

INCOMING KINDNESS

*If anyone has material possessions and sees a
brother or sister in need but has no pity on them,
how can the love of God be in that person?*

I JOHN 3:17 NIV

*W*hen she opened her inbox, her jaw dropped at the number of new emails awaiting her attention. Scrolling through them, searching for the ones relevant to her work and purchases, a subject heading pleading for help caught her attention. She hesitated. She'd seen these kinds of requests almost daily, and she'd learned to turn a blind eye to most of them. But she trusted the ministry requesting aid and clicked to find out the problem.

Once she read about the five-year drought ravaging Kenya and the surrounding countries, coupled with the fact that Christians there faced persecution that further complicated their access to lifesaving food and supplies, she couldn't unsee the need. She understood that while she sat comfortably at her computer, other Christians in the world were fighting for their lives—and she had a chance to help. Her offering seemed so small against such an overwhelming problem, but she trusted her Savior to turn her proverbial "five loaves and two fish" into something significant that could help relieve their suffering.

Compassion and kindness toward others in their time of need come from the heart of Jesus Christ. He sees and knows the situations in your life, your neighborhood, your city, state, country, and the world! While we can't possibly solve the world's problems on our own, God moves in our hearts through His Spirit to respond to the people He puts in our path—even when they show up in an inbox! God is at work all the time, and we experience His joy and purpose when we partner with Him, generously giving the time, talent, and treasures He has generously given to us. As we respond with prayer and practical support for the poor and needy, whether they are around the world or right next door, we please our Father who sees us walking in His footsteps.

Lord Jesus, please forgive my tendency to just take care of myself and my family and forget about others. Tune my spirit to Yours so that I see the needs around me and respond with the compassion and kindness of Christ. In Jesus's name.

HONEY'S CONSISTENCY

Kind words are like honey—
sweet to the soul and healthy for the body.

PROVERBS 16:24 NLT

I'm ready to get rid of our cat." Her son looked serious as he approached his mom while she was doing the dishes.

Her eyebrows dipped downward, and a frown lined her face. "But you love that cat. Why would you ever say anything like that?" she inquired, puzzled by his about-face affections.

"I'm just tired of the way she randomly tries to attack me!" he said. He then explained how when he'd go to pet her, she'd always start purring, nuzzle his hand, and rub her body around his legs. "She acts like she likes me but then *Wham!* Out of nowhere she just decides to take a chunk out of my hand!" He held out two wounded hands for her to inspect.

Seeing the puncture wounds and blood, she also saw his point. It's hard to cuddle or even be kind to a creature whose loyalties and temper seem so fickle.

The same goes for people too. We all know people whose short fuse leads to loud outbursts and angry tirades that leave those in their wake feeling deeply wounded. They may be fun and jovial much of the time, but the sporadic nature of their caustic behavior makes us cautious about continuing any level of friendship. We can all be like that fickle cat or volatile friend sometimes.

But God calls His kids to be different. He wants the words of our mouth and the meditations of our heart to be pleasing in His sight (Psalm 19:14). When we allow the Spirit of God to search our souls and show us where darkness is lurking within, we can confess it and replace it with the truth and grace from God's Word and ask for help in walking it out. By leaning into the Spirit, we can consistently offer the kind of words that build others up, even when in the midst of conflict. Christ's patience and kindness toward us teach us the way to maintain our witness and bring life into all of our conversations.

Lord Jesus, I want to honor You with what I say and do. Show me where I may be harboring bitterness or unforgiveness and help me let go of it. Fill me with Your everlasting kindness so that my words will bring life to others too. In Jesus's name.

ONLY ONE

And Jesus said to him, "Why do you call me good? No one is good except God alone."

MARK 10:18 ESV

Normally, she loved to host, but her empty fridge and her friends' last-minute change of plans left her scrambling for a dinner idea. Quickly she ran to the store and grabbed some meat and corn to throw on the grill and a basket of strawberries to top the pound cake for dessert.

But at home, her hope sank. As she took a closer look at her purchases, she let out a long, frustrated sigh. The meat she had selected was a week past the due date, and the top layer of strawberries hid a blanket of fuzzy white mold underneath, making every single berry useless. Nothing was salvageable. She felt a little sick to her stomach as she looked at the waste. "What can I do?" she wondered. Then she picked up the phone to order pizza instead.

It's a daunting moment when we realize that, despite all our good intentions, our efforts are as useless as that ruined food. We dare not try to force the matter, ingesting what we know would be rancid and toxic. But when it comes to spiritual matters, we often make that very same mistake. Somehow, we begin to think that we can transform the sinful nature we inherited as humans and make ourselves into good people. We try harder and harder, comparing ourselves to others in a flailing attempt to feel better about our own efforts but always wondering if it's good enough.

Jesus settles the question in Scripture. No one is good. Not even one person. Not the best person you know. No one is good but One, Jesus says, and that is God. Our only hope to become truly good people is to connect with the One who is. In a supernatural turn of events, when we surrender our sinful, spoiled selves to Christ, He infuses us with His Spirit of real righteousness and goodness. A resurrection in our spirit takes place, and the potential to work goodness into our world springs forth.

Lord God, You alone are good, and I praise You for Your righteousness and grace, given generously to sinners like me. Change me from the inside out and pour out Your goodness through me. In Jesus's name.

BUOYED BY GRACE

Do not be overcome by evil,
but overcome evil with good.
ROMANS 12:21 ESV

As he watched the instructional videos, he was mesmerized. A young girl flailed frantically in the water, screaming for help as she battled the waves and the hidden current that was causing her visible crisis. But as the lifeguard swam out to meet her, she didn't relax or act relieved at all, despite her savior's arrival. Instead, the panic and thrashing only intensified. "You can't approach someone drowning from the front," the instructor called out to the class over the video. "Watch how the lifeguard comes in from behind." Sure enough, he swam around the girl to get to the back where he could reach under her armpits and secure her shoulders while protecting himself from her frantic gestures. Buoyed by the life preserver he brought, they both made it to shore safely and swiftly.

In a very real way, God calls His kids to be lifeguards for a world full of people in danger of drowning in spiritual darkness. Most of the time, they know they're in some sort of trouble—their souls endlessly searching for an identity or purpose to cling to for life. But finding no solid or stable ground, they

begin flailing and grasping at whatever promises to change their fate. Unfortunately, even Christians can find themselves in a similar state if they wander away from the safety of Truth's shore.

But we must be careful with our approach to rescuing. If we barge in with a frontal attack, seeking to forcefully rip the wrong idols out of their hands, the struggle may sink us both. Instead, we grab hold of the Spirit of God to buoy us with His grace and truth. We surprise them with the radical kindness and security of God's love, extended to them in spite of their oppositional defiance. Through prayer and persistent goodness, we work in tandem with God's ever-present Spirit and His timing to pull them back to safety.

Lord, thank You for rescuing me from certain death. I am awed by Your goodness and want to extend that to others, even if they only retaliate against my efforts. Help me to overcome evil with good, acting toward others out of the overflow of Your mercy toward me. In Jesus's name.

IN HOT PURSUIT

*Surely Your goodness and love will follow me
all the days of my life, and I will dwell
in the house of the LORD forever.*

PSALM 23:6 NIV

She had seen him shopping in the same department store but hadn't thought anything of it. But now on the busy streets of New York City, she saw him again, this time making direct eye contact. It seemed he was trying to weave his way through the crowds to get to her. Uncertain of his intentions and unnerved by his pursuit, she quickened her pace, occasionally glancing back to see if he was gone. But he was gaining ground!

So she started to run, strangers gawking at her stride, seeing the man closing in now and shouting for her attention. Realizing she was running out of steam and simply couldn't outpace him, she turned on her heels to face her stalker head-on. Out of breath, he ran to her, slowing down as he approached. "Ma'am"—he stalled between breaths—"you sure are fast. But I'm glad I finally caught you." He held up her wallet. "You left this in the store, and I was afraid someone would steal it."

Dumbfounded by his determination to help her despite all her efforts to avoid him, she finally smiled.

"I thought you were out to get me!" She offered an embarrassed laugh, taking the wallet. "But thank you for chasing me down!"

It's scary when we think we're being watched or even chased. We fear for our lives. Unfortunately, we can sometimes feel that way about God. We may even secretly believe He's just out to get us.

But when we finally encounter Jesus, we realize how wrong we were! While it's true that God hates sin, He loves His people with a passion we can't even comprehend. It's why He sent Jesus to save us from our sins and the curse they bring—so that we can be free and whole and reconciled to Him for the rest of eternity. God's mercy and goodness pursue us to bless our lives with all the wonder and hope that intimacy with our Creator brings.

Father, please forgive me for sometimes thinking that You don't have my best interests at heart. I believe that You are always good, and You are working out everything in my life for my good. Free me to receive from You so that I can bless others. In Jesus's name.

NOT ALONE

Then the Lord God said,
"It is not good for the man to be alone.
I will make a helper who is right for him.""

GENESIS 2:18 NCV

A hush fell across the crowd as the couple skated their way to the center of the rink and assumed their starting pose like two statues. After a few seconds' pause, music sounded through the loudspeaker, summoning the sculptures to life as they glided across the ice. With what looked like hardly an effort, the male skater hoisted his partner above his head, only one arm securing her graceful body as they soared across the rink in a large semicircle. Then suddenly, she dropped down, caught in his waiting arms as the fluid motion never wavered for a moment. Spin after death-defying spin always led the couple back to one another, the two moving as one even when time and space separated them for a few moments. With every expression and the ending embrace, grace and beauty flowed across the vast white ice, mesmerizing everyone who watched in awestruck approval. Their performance landed them a near-perfect score and a standing ovation.

Isn't it beautiful to watch unity like that in motion? God certainly thinks so. He tells us in His Word that the

watching world will actually begin to believe in Jesus when we love others well and work together in unity (John 17:21). From the very beginning of time before sin ever entered the picture, God declared that all of His creation was good except for one thing: Adam was alone. But in creating Eve, the isolation ended, and the two became one as they worked and lived under God's care. And God said it was "very good."

Now, thousands of years later, God's declaration remains the same. We weren't made to live alone in our own private worlds. God welcomes us into His family where we find brothers and sisters in Christ who help us carry out our mission to know Jesus and make Him known. As we learn to both lead and follow in love, our skeptical world will notice the difference and want to know the source of such goodness.

Jesus, thank You for calling me into community with You and Your people. Help me to guard against isolating myself, and help me stay connected with others in Your peace and love. In Jesus's name.

DO-GOODERS

Therefore, as we have opportunity, let us do good to all people, especially to those who belong to the family of believers.

GALATIANS 6:10 NIV

*A*cross the country, millions of Americans awoke to the tragic news. In the night hours, a series of long-range tornadoes tore across the southern states, leaving a wide swath of devastation everywhere they touched. Homes and churches and buildings lay decimated. Debris, broken trees, and downed power lines littered entire counties. It looked like the apocalypse, with too much destruction for the dazed and confused survivors to even comprehend.

But storm chasers and other onlookers reported the scene to the rest of the world. Soon, everyone tuning in marveled in awe and wondered what it would be like to live through something so instantly catastrophic. Most just inwardly winced as they took in the news, glad it wasn't their town. In time, they went on with their day.

Truth is, we wake up to stories of hurt and heartache every day. From mass shootings to riots, freak accidents to intentional evil, we are inundated with the awful news that our world is in shambles, and we shake our heads at its brokenness. Sometimes it feels so overwhelming, we are tempted to drown out the darkness with whatever we can find to distract or numb us.

But as believers, we don't have to just watch in despair. Instead of shaking our heads in hopelessness, we lift our eyes to the heavens where our help comes from. Our very bodies house the greatness and glory of our God, and He gives us entrance into His throne room in heaven whenever and wherever we go. As His living temple filled with His light, we can instantly bring the broken and hurting before Him in prayer, pleading for their help and relief. Then when the Spirit responds to us, we have the opportunity to act. Just like Jesus, we enter into the mess with the hope and help of the Father. Like Jesus, we get to roll up our sleeves and offer a helping hand, encouraging word, or timely hug to ease the hurt. We can weather the difficulty because we never walk alone. And when we reach out to others to bless them in Jesus's name, we usher His brilliant light into the night, leading others to take refuge in Him too.

Jesus, I don't want to be like the world that despairs in these dark times. I look to You for strength and direction. Please guide my heart to pray and feet to walk in Your good works. In Jesus's name.

THE GREAT ESCAPE

Finally, brothers and sisters, whatever is true, whatever is noble, whatever is right, whatever is pure, whatever is lovely, whatever is admirable—if anything is excellent or praiseworthy—think about such things.

PHILIPPIANS 4:8 NIV

*I*t took a bit of effort to get there, but the moment finally arrived. She opened up her beach chair facing the lapping waves of the Emerald Coast and sank down on the sand, legs extending into the cool waters. As the warmth and water washed over her, the weight of the world lifted off her shoulders. She couldn't help but smile as her senses drank in the delightful blue skies with seagulls and pelicans flying overhead and endless white sands stretching along the shoreline. The scene worked its magic every time, erasing the stress and concerns of life and allowing her mind a moment of bliss.

Isn't relief the reason we all want a vacation? If even for a day, we dream and plan for a time when we can just get away from the craziness of the world and unwind. But did you know that God invites us to get away *every* day? While retreats are necessary for deep restoration, God's presence shelters us from the storms and stress of life every single time we come to Him through prayer and meditation on His

goodness. And when we fix our minds on Him and all the wonderful benefits we share simply by belonging to Him, His truth and love transform our thoughts from darkness and despair to beauty and light that shine brighter than the Florida sun.

Vacations are good, but living day to day resting in the goodness of God is even better. It prepares us to handle the events of the day with hope and grace as we feed our minds with good, God-centered thoughts. And resting in God's goodness positions us to shine like the sun in a dark world that desperately needs to know the Way of escape: Jesus Himself.

Lord, sometimes I catch myself spiraling downward in dark thoughts when I focus on the problems I see around me, or watch and listen to messages that burden me. I choose to lift my eyes up to You. Allow Your warmth and goodness to restore my anxious thoughts and lead me to rest. In Jesus's name.

PANNING
FOR GOLD

Don't just pretend to love others.
Really love them. Hate what is wrong.
Hold tightly to what is good.
ROMANS 12:9 NLT

It was Pioneer Week at Oakland Elementary, and all the third graders were giddy with excitement. Today, they'd be panning for gold in a makeshift creek bed the teachers created to simulate the practice during California's Gold Rush days. To make their quest successful, the teachers stocked the mud troughs with tons of hidden gems before the children arrived. At last, the students all lined up, ready for the day's adventure.

"Here are your gold pans," one teacher called out over the clamor as she got their attention. "When it's your turn, dig up a panful of the dirt and rocks. You won't see any gems right away," she explained. "Next, take your pan over to the water where you'll submerge your pan and gently shake it back and forth until all the dirt washes away. Then you'll be able to see where any gold or other gems are hiding. And you can keep whatever you find!"

All the kids clapped enthusiastically.

Who doesn't love a successful treasure hunt?

As believers living in a sin-sick world, we are given the opportunity to search for the treasures of God's goodness every single day. Like the elementary school teachers, God has already stocked His Word and world with invaluable truth that both saves and sustains our lives. But in Scripture, He also warns us about the dirty tricks of Satan, our enemy, who is described as the craftiest of God's creation and the father of lies. He can even appear as an angel of light, the proverbial wolf in sheep's clothing.

So how can we sift through all the strong and convincing opinions of this world to find what's actually true? God says we need to pan for His gold. Run the water of His Word over every message we hear before we decide to keep it and believe it. Let go of the bad. Cling to what is good and right and true. And the God of all goodness will enrich Your life with His divine wisdom.

Father, You have promised that when I seek You with all my heart, I will find You. Help me to sift through every opinion and teaching I encounter and test it according to Your Word. I want to cling to You no matter what the world around me says. In Jesus's name.

THE FANATIC

*"Neither do people light a lamp
and put it under a bowl.
Instead they put it on its stand, and
it gives light to everyone in the house.
In the same way, let your light shine
before others, that they may see
your good deeds and
glorify your Father in heaven."*

MATTHEW 5:15-16 NIV

The new hire left no doubts where his passions lay. From day one in the office, he decked out his cubicle with different memorabilia from his favorite football team—the team's traditional crimson and white coloring the flags, photos, and signed football sitting on his shelf. But his passion wasn't just reserved for display. At break time, he found others in the office who shared his affinity for football and engaged them in lively discussions about coaching trends, recent swaps, and future predictions for the coming weekend. His steady enthusiasm and outspoken interest eventually inspired the entire office to join in the fun of choosing a team and cheering for their success, even coworkers who had never been a fan of any sport before!

A true football fanatic sets their sights on every

possible way to support their team and tell others about it in the process. It's impressive to see such passion on display, particularly in the stadium where thousands of like-minded fans unite together to cheer their team to victory.

As believers, we have a cause far greater than any other team on earth. When we are living for Jesus and deeply devoted to Him and His kingdom growth, we can't keep it contained. The enthusiasm and energy overflows everywhere we go—at work, at school, at home, even in the grocery store. And at church, we gather together with other fellow Christ-fans and shout His praises in song and Word when we're together, letting the whole world know that we don't just live for weekends, we live for eternity. Don't let the naysayers sabotage your spirit. Set your affections on Jesus and watch His passion within you win a watching world to Him.

Lord, I'm so excited to belong to You and be a part of Your family. I don't want to keep my joy and passion to myself! Today, give me opportunities to share with others what all You've done for me and the great hope we have in You for the future. Let them see the goodness of the Lord too! In Jesus's name.

BURNING QUESTIONS

"For the mouth speaks what the heart is full of.
A good man brings good things
out of the good stored up in him,
and an evil man brings evil things
out of the evil stored up in him."

MATTHEW 12:34-35 NIV

It had been a wonderful day at the beach, and now her husband stood in the kitchen cooking up her favorite corn and lobster bisque. As she and the whole family sat on the condo's balcony enjoying the steady breeze and casual conversation, they'd occasionally catch the savory smell of fresh herbs and other seasonings that made the dish an easy success every time. But suddenly her husband started shouting, "No, no, no, nooooo!" They all looked inside to see what was happening. He seemed frantic.

"What's wrong?" they all wanted to know.

"It burned!" he moaned. "The whole pot is ruined." His shoulders sagged. "We're going to have to throw it all out."

"Surely it can't *all* be bad. Let me taste," his wife encouraged. Immediately she knew he was right. By leaving his post for the few minutes it took to prepare a side dish, he'd left the heat on too high, and in an instant the scorched bottom permeated the entire pot.

Isn't it frustrating when something meant to be so good goes bad?

God agrees and gives us great direction to keep the goodness going. Like that pot of bisque, our souls simmer with the ingredients we pour into it. If we're not careful, daily ingestion of toxic worldly messages can become beliefs that singe your whole soul with the stench of evil. So we need to be diligent to stir up our spirit and ask: Are we meditating on the promises of God and cultivating a thankful heart? Are we keeping short accounts and being quick to forgive so no bitter roots poison the roux? Are we staying in sync with God's Spirit, keeping our sights on His plan and purpose? If so, the savory mix will waft into the world through our conversation and daily lives, blessing everyone around us who is hungry for life-giving encouragement.

Father, You have given me everything I need for life and godliness—and it is very good. Help me to guard against worldly input and stinking thinking. Thank You, too, that Your forgiveness restores and makes me new. Nothing is ruined in Your hands! In Jesus's name.

RIGHT NOW

Yet I am confident
I will see the LORD's goodness
while I am here in the land of the living.

PSALM 27:13 NLT

*H*e had been planning this day for weeks, hoping to strengthen the bond with his moody, tween-aged daughter. Knowing her love for Asian cuisine and culture, he called ahead to a renowned sushi restaurant and made reservations. After lunch, he'd take her to the nearby botanical gardens where the sakura trees should be in full, beautiful bloom. Finally, he figured they'd end their adventures at her favorite boba tea café, where they could also play board games and hopefully get some good conversation going.

But right off the bat, he noticed something was wrong. His daughter seemed distracted and distant during the car ride to lunch. Conversation at the restaurant seemed equally difficult as she texted on her phone and complained about the menu's offerings. And though for a moment the trees in the garden got her smile of approval, shortly thereafter she began asking when they could go home.

"What's the matter?" her dad finally confronted his sullen daughter. "I'm really wanting to enjoy this

day with you."

"Uh, yeah. I know. It's nice, Dad," she acknowledged but added, "I just can't wait until tomorrow. It's going to be great! All of my friends are getting together, and we're going to hang out at my best friend's house."

What was his daughter's problem? It certainly wasn't his planning or provision. Instead, it was her perspective! She couldn't see the beauty before her because she kept looking longingly to the future, forfeiting the day's fun and intimacy with her father.

Unfortunately, we can make the same mistake. God our Father wants us to see the beauty of His purpose and plan that He's packed into our present moment, not just in the future. As our spiritual sight grows accustomed to recognizing His hand at work in every detail of our lives, we begin looking even harder for the doors He opens for us to join Him in kingdom work. With His Spirit leading, our hearts fill with gratitude for His grace in each moment, even as we long for the day when we'll see Him and all of God's family face-to-face.

Lord, I don't want to miss You today. Open my eyes to see and my ears to hear Your love and leadership in my life. Thank You for wanting to spend time with me and walking with me day by day! In Jesus's name.

TAKE ME BACK

Lord, I have heard of Your fame;
I stand in awe of Your deeds, Lord.
Repeat them in our day,
in our time make them known;
in wrath remember mercy.

HABAKKUK 3:2 NIV

She tugged on the rope and pulled down hard as the wooden ladder unfolded from the attic door. Climbing up to the top, she surveyed the attic and its collection of memorabilia stored and forgotten from long ago. Slowly, she worked her way around the space, inspecting old dolls and clothes and other odds and ends until she came to her old record player and albums. "Oh, I remember these," she mused out loud, turning the albums over to recall which songs they contained. Finding the only outlet, she plugged in the record player and laid the vinyl on the spinning plate. She gently put the needle in place.

Instantly, music flooded the dusty room, filling the dreary deadness with a surprising jolt of life. "Man, that takes me back!" she marveled as memories from long ago rose to the surface of her mind and she smiled, soaking in the warmth of yesteryear. She sang each line as if no time had passed, the melody

still holding the magic that set her soul free.

It's kind of crazy how music settles in our memory and aids in unlocking the past. Maybe it's one of the reasons the psalmists recorded God's deeds in lyric form and sang them in times of worship.

We are a people who tend to forget even the good that happens in our lives. But God wants us to remember! He records His faithfulness in the pages of Scripture so that we can look back at His proven character when we're questioning life in the present. Throughout history, God's record rings flawless and true, and inspires us to trust Him no matter what we encounter.

Take time today to reflect on all the ways God has shown His faithfulness in ages past as well as in your own lifetime. Let the memories and current reality of His steadfast love set your soul free to worship in wonder at how great is our God!

Lord, I will not forget Your mercy and grace toward me. You've proven Yourself again and again, and I plan to put Your praise on repeat for the rest of my days. In Jesus's name.

UNDER HIS CARE

Faithful is He who calls you, and He also will bring it to pass.

I THESSALONIANS 5:24 NASB1995

As her chickens scratched and pecked at the ground, she smiled. She knew they were happiest outside in the yard where they were free to fly and run and eat and roost—all the good habits of healthy chickens. She kept them well-watered and fed, protected by a large cage to keep out any predators. Having raised them from chicks, she watched them grow into the plump mother birds they were, each with her own peculiarities and personality. In the safety of their surroundings, the hens daily laid eggs that she enjoyed gathering and offering to family and friends for a farm-fresh breakfast.

As ordinary as the scene was, she couldn't help but see some spiritual significance in the simplicity of farm life. Good owners take all the worry away by predicting their animals' needs and providing accordingly so their furry or feathered friends can thrive. No fretting, complaining, or comparing required!

Jesus relays the same thought when He reminds His followers that God watches over all His creation so closely that He even notices when a single bird falls

to the ground. *And you are worth much more than the sparrow!* (Luke 12:6-7). Unlike any other creature on earth, our heavenly Father created us to live and love and thrive on earth as His treasured children, expressing our individuality in full community with Jesus and the Holy Spirit.

We are sheltered under His watchful care and can be confident that nothing comes into our lives that He doesn't allow for our own good. Therefore we are free to enjoy the beauty of life moment by moment. No fretting, complaining, or comparing required—our Savior and Lord has seen to our every need, providing exactly what we need to live well for Him right where we are. He is faithful to take care of us so that we can live authentic lives full of unique personality and purpose that make our Father smile with delight.

Father, You know all the days ordained for me before even one comes to be. I surrender my efforts to fix myself and my circumstances. I yield to Your care and trust You to grow me, and all You love, up into mature followers who reflect Your faithful love. In Jesus's name.

BOUND TOGETHER

Let love and faithfulness never leave you;
bind them around your neck,
write them on the tablet of your heart.
Then you will win favor and a good name
in the sight of God and man.

PROVERBS 3:3-4 NIV

She couldn't quit staring at her ring finger as she rubbed the space where her wedding band was supposed to be. "I should have never taken it off," she scolded herself for removing her ring the night before as she cleaned the dishes. Somehow in cleaning off the counter's clutter, her ring was knocked off the ledge and fell right down the drain. She rubbed the empty indentation at her finger's base and sighed. Decades of wear had worn a deep groove into her skin that stayed, despite the loss, and signaled a lifetime of love and commitment...of undying devotion. Picking up the phone, she called the plumber for help. No matter what the cost, she couldn't let the precious reminder of love remain lost. It had become a part of who she was!

We wear symbols such as wedding rings to remind us of whose we are and the commitment we've made to one another. It sends a signal to

us and others that we have a unique and binding relationship with another person that establishes the boundaries, patterns, and purpose for our lives.

In a similar way, God's Spirit is His sign to us that we belong to Him, His guarantee that we will be with Him forever. Whether we lie down in sleep or wake to face a new day, our faithful Friend goes wherever we do, reminding us of Whose we are. Yet even when we forsake His affections and make sinful choices, God's faithfulness never wavers. Like the grooves on the bride's finger, God's presence in us makes an indelible imprint in our souls. He is faithful even when we are not. We never stop being His. But when we sin, His Spirit reminds us to simply call on Jesus—the One who restores our hearts and minds and souls. His forgiveness is swift, and His love endures forever. Great is His faithfulness!

Jesus, You are my faithful Husband and Friend. I'm thrilled to belong to You, and I want the world to see the beautiful relationship we have. Please help me to honor You by living a life of faithful reliance on You, even as You faithfully take care of me. I love You! In Jesus's name.

MOVING MOUNTAINS

He replied, "Because you have so little faith. Truly I tell you, if you have faith as small as a mustard seed, you can say to this mountain, 'Move from here to there,' and it will move. Nothing will be impossible for you."

MATTHEW 17:20 NIV

The young boy stood mesmerized as he watched the construction crew maneuver their colossal machines in tandem to achieve their plan. Weeks ago, marking sticks had lined the landscape behind their house, indicating where pipes and plots would one day be placed in the new subdivision being developed just beyond the boy's backyard fence.

The bulldozers, excavators, and dump trucks were working steadily to shift the scene, creating new drainage systems and roadways as they went. But what held his attention today was the large hill that once rested close behind his home. Steadily, the excavator extended its neck, scooping earth up into its giant metal bucket. It swung around smoothly where the dump truck waited for its load. Once full, the excavator beeped, sending the truck on its way and making room for the next one in line. With precision teamwork, the crew dug away layer after layer until the small mountain was no more. Then they

leveled the area, forming the foundations where new homes would be built.

It is truly amazing what consistent, steady work coupled with powerful engines can produce. The construction crew literally moves mountains as a regular part of their jobs. Jesus tells us that His true followers possess the same potential when we partner up with His powerful Spirit. All it takes is a vision for His plan and persistent faith that as we keep following God, He will accomplish the work.

What in your life seems insurmountable today? Is it a difficult boss? Insufficient funds? A haunting past? Or personal relationship problems? Don't be discouraged by what you see with your eyes. Look with your heart to the One Whose outstretched arm is mighty to save in ways your mind can't even conceive. Like the construction crew, partner up with other believers who share the same kingdom purpose. Then press into prayer on a moment-by-moment basis, believing that God is working in tandem with your petitions. In His time, the mountain will topple, and you will see clearly the firm foundation of trust He was building into you all along.

Lord, I will not be discouraged by situations that seem hopeless, because nothing is impossible with You! You are my Helper and my God who moves mountains, and I will persist in faithful prayer as I watch You move. In Jesus's name.

OUR ONLY HOPE

Faith means being sure of the things we hope for
and knowing that something is real
even if we do not see it.
Faith is the reason we remember
great people who lived in the past.

HEBREWS 11:1-2 NCV

She had thought it through and settled on her decision. Ever since she saw the scans, she knew she lived on borrowed time. The tumor in her brain grew bigger every day, and her doctor warned her not to delay. Still, the terror of brain surgery and the awkward sedation they used for it paused her consent. She researched alternative options only to find surgical removal was her only hope.

Fortunately, in her searching, she also uncovered more information about her surgeon. Scores of five-star reviews followed after his name. Many patients who underwent the same procedure were now healed and singing his praises.

"There's really no other option," she finally told her husband, affirming her decision to proceed. "I'm going forward because I'll die if I don't. And from all that I've read and heard, he's the best surgeon for the job."

Faith—the kind that moves us forward to action—

doesn't have to be blind. God can handle every question and concern we have. He urges us to study the Scriptures where we will find the truth about who He has been throughout history and always will be. We can be confident in His promises and care!

Just as the young woman researched her options, God gives us grace to ask the kind of questions we need to learn about His character, which He clearly reveals in His Word. Other people's testimonies of His faithfulness in their lives fuel our feeble faith as well, often fanning it into flame. But with life-crushing sin crouching at our door, we dare not wait. Today and every day, let us entrust ourselves to His capable care—even when it means cutting out intrusive thoughts, habits, or relationships that threaten our spiritual well-being. His surgeon's knife is our saving grace.

Like the disciple Peter said, "Lord, to whom shall we go? You have the words of eternal life, and we have believed, and have come to know, that you are the Holy One of God" (John 6:68-69, ESV).

Jesus, thank You for allowing me the freedom to speak openly and honestly with You, even in my fear and doubt. Please strengthen my faith as I willingly give You full control over my life. In Jesus's name.

LOOKING UP

My heart, O God, is steadfast;
I will sing and make music with all my soul.
Awake, harp and lyre!
I will awaken the dawn.
I will praise You, Lord, among the nations;
I will sing of You among the peoples.
For great is Your love, higher than the heavens;
Your faithfulness reaches to the skies.

PSALM 108:1-4 NIV

She tightened her seat belt and gripped the handrests as she listened intently to the flight attendant's instructions. It was her first time in an airplane, and the idea of hurtling through the sky in an enormous steel contraption seemed more than counterintuitive. Her stomach churned in protest. She was terrified!

As the plane pulled out onto the tarmac, she watched out the window. Suddenly, the engines revved, and the plane gained speed, rolling then lifting then flying up into the sky. Soon the people and buildings below shrank out of sight as the plane flew upward through the low-lying cloud cover into beautiful blue skies above. As the plane leveled off, so did her anxiety. "I'm in the heavens!" she smiled to herself, relaxing her grip and releasing her breath. Up

so high, it felt like another world. "Even here, You're still with me," she whispered a prayer, her fearful thoughts coming full circle to praise.

King David never flew in a plane, but he could relate to her lofty realization: God is greater than our wildest imagination. His love is stronger than the sun. And His faithfulness stretches higher than the heavens! We might not be able to wrap our minds around that level of goodness, but we get a glimpse of it through the physical world God has made. The heavens were the highest point in the psalmist's vocabulary, the greatest scale he could capture in words. But God's faithfulness stretches even farther.

The next time you find yourself stressing out or overcome with worry, take a walk outside. Look up at the skies and let the vast expanse remind you just how big and wise and powerful our God is. Then remember that the same God who made those skies sees you and promises to never leave your side. Rest in His faithfulness!

Lord, I can't even comprehend how much You love me. I never need to be afraid because I know You surround me and fill me with Your sweet presence, my never-ending source of peace. I praise You because Your faithfulness reaches higher than the heavens! In Jesus's name.

MORNING ROUTINE

***Because of the Lord's great love we are not
consumed, for His compassions never fail. They are
new every morning; great is Your faithfulness.***

LAMENTATIONS 3:22-23 NIV

From her bed, she could hear the clank and shuffle of her dog's food bowl. She didn't even have to see him to know he was nosing it around, intentionally banging it against the floor and cabinets until she came to fill it up. It was just a part of their daily routine.

So she rolled out of bed, grabbed her robe and slippers, and walked over to her dog who looked up longingly in eager expectation. She reached down to pet his head, but he turned his face toward the bowl, signifying his priorities. She laughed and patted him anyway and then filled up his food and water bowls. By the time she poured her own cup of coffee and sat down on the couch for her morning devotions, he had already finished and jumped up to snuggle against her robe—her favorite part of their morning ritual.

Wouldn't life be wonderful if people were as dependable as our pets? We love to dote on them every day because their warm, fuzzy fur and love-filled licks bring such joy and comfort into our lives.

We don't begrudge their dependency on us; we enjoy it! Our pets provide an awesome outlet for our affections and desire for companionship.

In a similar way as our furry friends, we awake each day in desperate need of our Father's care. But we don't have to make a lot of noise to get His attention. We simply need to turn our hearts toward Him in prayer! Every single day, He delights in cleaning out yesterday's problems and preparing our hearts to receive His new mercies and grace, poured out through His Spirit. In the exchange, we're not only nourished, but we're also invited to cuddle up close beside our Master, Savior, and Friend and simply enjoy the miraculous moment of His making this day new. It's a routine we can rely on for the rest of our lives until we're brought into permanent and perfect relationship with Jesus in heaven.

Lord, thank You for never getting tired of taking care of me. Every morning I can get up knowing I'm completely loved because You never fail to forgive and take care of me. You are my favorite resting place! In Jesus's name.

THE WAY OUT

No temptation has overtaken you
that is not common to man.
God is faithful, and he will not let you
be tempted beyond your ability,
but with the temptation he will also
provide the way of escape,
that you may be able to endure it.

I CORINTHIANS 10:13 ESV

He hadn't meant to splinter off from the group of hikers exploring the far side of the valley. But he'd heard a curious call and ventured out beyond the campsite to find what animal it could be. Suddenly, he saw a large bald eagle soaring overhead and wondered where it might land. *Maybe I can find the nest*, he thought as he kept tracking the large bird as it flew from tree to tree. But after an hour of pursuit, the eagle flew out of sight, and he realized his dilemma: he was lost, it was almost night, and his impulsive exploration left him unprepared. His only hope was the small compass he always carried in his pocket. Following its directional arrow, he headed due north. He knew that eventually he'd reach the main road and could find his way out of the wilderness and back to camp.

We all live in a world where it's easy to get off

course. Just one wrong online click can take us down a dark and dangerous path where we never meant to go. The same applies to the friends we choose and the other ways we spend our time. The deviation may seem innocent enough at first, but Scripture warns that if we persist in pursuing sin, it leads to death.

But God is faithful to help us in our weakness every time we ask. He provides a way out through the power of His Spirit and the encouragement of Christian community. Like a compass, God's provision points to the way out of deception or destruction and back home toward truth and communion with Him. Whenever you're tempted to stray, cry out to God for help and look to His Word for the true north. Then walk in His ways to return home safe and sound.

Jesus, You were tempted in every way that we are, yet You never sinned. I know that You understand my struggle and are strong in me to help me overcome it. Lord, help me, in Jesus's name!

AGE TO AGE

*"Even to your old age and gray hairs I am He,
I am He who will sustain you.
I have made you and I will carry you;
I will sustain you and I will rescue you."*

ISAIAH 46:4 NIV

The cashier didn't mean to depress her. It's just that in applying a senior citizen discount without even asking, the middle-aged woman realized that her aging showed. At home, she stopped by the bathroom mirror for a closer look. Yep, the gray hairs she had colored a few weeks ago had rebelliously burst through again at the roots. A once supple and smooth face now sported age spots and freckles amid an ever-growing mountain range of wrinkles under her eyes and on her forehead. She sighed and allowed her thoughts to drift back and forth: to the past, remembering how her body used to look… and to the future, wondering what would become of her in the end. "Charm is deceptive, and beauty is fleeting; but a woman who fears the LORD is to be praised," she quoted Proverbs 31:30 (NIV) out loud to quell her concerns. Still, it was hard to let go of the idols of youth. *What will happen when I'm really old?* she wondered.

Then she heard God's Spirit whisper another

reminder of His faithfulness: "Even to your old age and gray hairs I am He, I am He who will sustain you" (Isaiah 46:4 NIV). She didn't know what the future would hold, but she was grateful to know who was holding her.

Nothing in this world compares to the faithfulness of our God. He knew us before He laid the foundations of the world. He leads us through the ages and phases of our lives and never once leaves our side. He is the same yesterday, today, and forever—the firmest of foundations on which we can build our lives.

The clamor of our culture is to cling to youth with all the help money can buy—an obsession born of the fear that we will outgrow our purpose and worth. But God's unfailing love and everlasting care proves our infinite worth, no matter how old we are or how much our skin sags. In Jesus, we are chosen and cherished from life's first cry to final breath. Great is His faithfulness!

Jesus, You are the Great I Am, and You always will be. You alone determine my worth, not the color of my hair or condition of my physical body. Thank You for Your promise to stay with me, even to the end of the age. In Jesus's name.

HANG ON

*Let us hold fast the confession
of our hope without wavering,
for He who promised is faithful.*

HEBREWS 10:23 NASB1995

Standing on the platform, it felt like she was on top of the world. A canopy of treetops stretched before her, lining the sloping mountainside into a valley far below. Just above her head, a cable gently swayed in the wind. "Here's your harness," the zipline director instructed. "I'm going to lock the carabiner in place here so that you're securely on the line all the way down to the bottom. Just hold onto this bar and have fun!" he explained as she stepped into the contraption that locked her in. Checking all the straps, he signaled for her to jump, trusting her life to the thin line holding her from above.

She was terrified at first, the pull of gravity and speed of the pulley stealing her breath for the first few seconds. But as her trust in her harness grew, she loosened her grip and began enjoying the ride, taking in the sky above and the earth below. Indeed, it was the ride of her life, an adrenaline-pumping experience that only ended when she reached the final platform far below.

Deciding to surrender our lives to Jesus can feel

a little bit like standing on that top zipline platform. Emotions are high and it feels like we're on top of the world. But entrusting our lives to someone we can't even see can be scary. If we're truly trusting God, He may lead us to people and places far outside our comfort zone in order to cultivate our character and accompany Him in kingdom work.

When we stay tethered to God's truth, we can continue through life with confidence not only that He's holding onto us, but also that we're headed straight for our final destination—our heavenly home with Him. This is the very reason Scripture encourages us to never lose hope. Abandoning our trust is like unhooking our harness midway through the course! Keep the faith by holding onto the hope of Jesus's promise. He is faithful and will see you through to the end!

Jesus, I never want to do life without You. Help me to cling to You as You lead me through life. I love the adventure You've laid out before Me. Help me to rest on the ride knowing You're the One holding me close. In Jesus's name.

LEADING LOWLY

"Take my yoke upon you and learn from Me,
for I am gentle and humble in heart, and
you will find rest for your souls."

MATTHEW 11:29 NIV

*I*magine getting word that the President of the United States had chosen your town for an upcoming visit. Rumors about his anticipated arrival would spread across the community and become talking points on every local news and radio station. People everywhere would be on the lookout for Air Force One or a long stretch limo surrounded by security to signal the time had come. We would expect law enforcement and our local government officials to be notified and prepared to offer a warm welcome and the best accommodations a small town could put together. It would be an exciting event to witness, even though we probably wouldn't get to interact with the distinguished leader personally.

In a similar way, the Jewish people of Jesus's day had anticipated the arrival of the promised Messiah sent to save them from their distress. Hundreds of prophecies in their ancient scrolls predicted the details surrounding His coming. So many people stayed on the lookout for a larger-than-life leader to appear.

But Jesus didn't arrive with an entourage or even local acclaim. God sovereignly chose His precious Son to be born in a stable, wrapped in swaddling clothes. He'd go on to grow up in a poor carpenter's family in the nondescript town of Nazareth. And for thirty years, Jesus lived in relative obscurity as He experienced everyday life on this planet. But once His public ministry began, the King of all Creation chose a ragtag team of mostly uneducated men as His disciples. People of ill-repute formed His biggest fan base. And He entered into the everyday pain and struggle of the people He came to save.

Far greater than any other authority this world has ever known, Jesus came not to be served but to serve. Unlike the other religious leaders who lorded their power over the people, His gentle and lowly disposition drew the despised and down-and-out to Him. When we let Christ's Spirit reign in us, we can do the same.

Jesus, I, too, am drawn to Your compassionate and gentle heart. You see deeply into our souls and love us just the same. Help me to walk in humility and gentleness, just like You. In Your name.

THE BEST BARGAIN

Let your gentle spirit
be known to all men.
The Lord is near.
PHILIPPIANS 4:5 NASB1995

The alarm clock sounded at 4:00 a.m., and she groaned, wondering why she had ever agreed to join her friend so early for the Black Friday specials. She hoped to score some bargains for Christmas, but she couldn't believe what she saw once she got to the store where she met her friend. A long line of hopeful shoppers snaked its way out the doors and deep into the dark parking lot. Through the store windows, they watched people wielding shopping carts like weapons as they tore down the aisles to reach the doorbusters first. Some shoppers began shoving, others resorted to shouting. Seeing the chaos, she commented, "What kind of insanity is this?! They're fighting over the silliest things!"

Then she announced a better idea. "We don't need to enter into that mess. We can get the best bargains online anyway—and they'll ship right to our door! Let's just go get some coffee instead."

Just like the friends, we have a choice to either enter into the world's way of fighting for place, power, and possessions, or lean on the Lord and learn

from Him. God's children are heirs of every spiritual blessing in the heavenly places. Whenever we are in a place of lack, we can simply ask our Father to provide, and He hears our prayers! We never have to fight or claw for position, compete to show our worth, or compare our lives against anyone else's. The world operates this way out of desperation for an identity that defines their worth. But we have our Creator God who calls us beloved, never leaves our side, and delights in lavishing His love and acceptance on His children. As the world clamors to advance their own self-interest, we can respond with gentleness because we've set our eyes on Jesus and we know that He's in control. We don't need to fear the future because He'll always be right there with us, keeping us close by His side.

Lord, sometimes I get caught up in the rat race of life, trying to make a name for myself and just get ahead. But I don't need or want that. I want to stay close to You and rest in Your provision so that my gentleness will be evident to all. In Jesus's name.

THE EXPERIMENT

A gentle answer turns away wrath,
but a harsh word stirs up anger.

PROVERBS 15:1 NIV

The science teacher stood at the front of the class and called the children to circle around the table. Everyone was curious about the large paper-mache volcano she had constructed and painted to look like an active volcano. She wanted them to witness firsthand how a chemical reaction plus pressure inside the volcano could result in an explosion of lava. First, she poured vinegar inside the crater and added a few drops of red dye. Next, she added a few drops of dishwashing detergent. "Now, class, watch what happens when we add just a little bit of baking soda." She poured some inside.

Almost instantly, red frothy "lava" shot out of the crater and poured down the sides of the makeshift mountain, a fountain of foam that just kept coming. "Why is so much more coming out than what we put in?" the kids wondered as they watched.

"It's the combustible nature of the chemicals we put inside the pressure chamber in the volcano's core," she explained.

In a similar way, Scripture tells us that the way we react to combustible situations has a powerful impact on what happens next. When other people wound us or say words meant to discourage or tear us down, it's tempting to lash back. Like adding baking soda to vinegar in the narrow chambers of our soul, scathing words and criticism come flowing out. Our anger escalates the dangerous or hurtful situation and can permanently damage everyone around us.

But God's Spirit enables us to diffuse a volatile situation through His gentle presence. He empowers us to respond to negativity with His dignity and grace. Because we are known and loved by God, we have a quiet confidence in Him that helps us see beyond a threatening situation to our Savior's kingdom purpose in that moment. By looking to Him for strength, we respond with a kindness that calms the storm of emotions and creates a better environment for healthy, life-giving conversation.

Lord, I don't want to be volatile like a volcano. I want Your Spirit of love and mercy to pour out of my mouth instead, bringing Your peace into every situation. Help me to turn to You before I blow my lid, and lead me in Your gentle ways. In Jesus's name.

LIVE OUT LOUD

But in your hearts revere Christ as Lord. Always be prepared to give an answer to everyone who asks you to give the reason for the hope that you have. But do this with gentleness and respect.

I PETER 3:15 NIV

*I*t had been a couple of years since the sales reps had last seen each other, but the regional sales conference brought them back. Together again, they took advantage of the break times to reconnect, and the conversations often turned lively. "You remember those girls we met at the bar that night?" Dave nudged Chuck with a knowing laugh. "Want to try our luck again this time?" he added, hoping to elicit some spontaneous adventure.

But instead, Chuck lowered his head and paused. Then, turning to face Dave, he braved telling him the truth about what had happened in his life. "I'm not the same guy you knew then," he began, relaying how his former way of life had led to some serious soul-searching. In his quest for meaning and purpose, he encountered Jesus. "And He changed everything."

Over the course of the next few days, Dave saw for himself the dramatic difference in Chuck. By the end, he couldn't keep his questions to himself any longer. "Listen, it looks like you're really onto something," he admitted. "Can we talk some more? You're the first Christian I've ever met who seems to be the real deal."

Unfortunately, many unsaved people have had negative experiences with religious people or hold harmful misperceptions about who God is. When we share our faith with them, we will gain more ground by first listening well, and *then* responding with gentleness and understanding to the hurts they've experienced and the questions they have. When someone knows we care about them, they'll be more open to hearing what we have to say, especially when they know we live out what we profess to believe. God's Word reminds us that it's the kindness of God that leads people to repentance. Let us be the kind of witnesses who represent the grace and patience of our Savior well. God's Spirit will take care of the rest!

Lord, help me to be ready to give an answer for why I've put my faith and hope in You. Open up doors for me to share my faith in a compelling way that leads others to You. In Jesus's name.

TRASH TALK

Remind them to be subject to rulers,
to authorities, to be obedient,
to be ready for every good deed,
to slander no one, not to be contentious,
to be gentle, showing every
consideration for all people.

TITUS 3:1-2 NASB

*H*e knew not to bring up politics at work. But in his mind, the car and home was another matter. Every day he'd leave the office tuned in to his favorite talk radio shows with hosts that he knew would support his perspective. Their stories and statistics fueled his conviction that he was right and the opposing party was dangerously wrong. By the time he got home, he'd post his opinions online where he felt free to fully vent his frustrations and judgments against all the political leaders that pulled the other way.

Unfortunately, political and spiritual polarization in our country threatens to divide and destroy us more than ever before. Even well-meaning Christians can get sucked into the aggressive hostility when they slam the people and opinions of others in an effort to support their side. But in the words of Martin Luther King, Jr., "Hate cannot drive out hate. Only love can do that."

Luther's words ring true because they're tied to Scripture. God's kingdom is not of this world, and He commands His kids to keep their attention on His interests, not what worries this world. When Jesus came to confront the wrong thinking and beliefs in His day, He did so with both truth and grace. He stood firmly on His Father's side while asking the kind of questions that made His opposers think and wrestle with their answers.

Jesus invites us to engage our world in the same manner. If we slander our leaders and put our opposers down in front of others, we're no different from the world. But if we lift up the truth of God's Word and speak life over those who follow His ways, we will wield greater influence. Empowered by His Spirit, we can help others get to the heart of their beliefs by asking the kind of questions that go beyond surface squabbles to trust and truth issues.

Father, my allegiance is to Your kingdom alone. I pray for our leaders that You will grant them wisdom in governing, and for Your people to drive out the hate in this country with Your love and truth. In Jesus's name.

GENTLE BLOOMS

Your beauty should not come from outward adornment,
such as elaborate hairstyles and the wearing of gold
jewelry or fine clothes. Rather, it should be that of
your inner self, the unfading beauty of a gentle and
quiet spirit, which is of great worth in God's sight.

I PETER 3:3-4 NIV

*W*hen she had looked up different ministry opportunities at her church, the Flower Ministry caught her eye. She'd help other women use leftover flowers from the Sunday pulpit floral spray to fill small vases that they'd take to a nearby nursing home.

Over time, she came to know each of the elderly residents. She learned about their life stories and the people of their past, along with their quirks and interests. But one of the women stood out from the rest. Betty's eyes lit up with joy every time the church volunteer walked in for a visit. With otherworldly acuity, the old woman always remembered her name and asked questions to keep current on what was happening in the young woman's life. More than anything, Betty loved to talk about Jesus, sharing the stories of her past that proved God's amazing faithfulness through her years. "Miss Betty," the weekly visitor often commented, "you help me more than I

help you! Your love for our Lord is more beautiful than the flowers I bring!"

God agrees! Gentle and quiet spirits reveal a deep trust in Jesus and a soul that is led by His Spirit. It's not an outward appearance or temperament determined by genetics; it's a result of day-by-day devotion to the Lord that tenderizes our hearts and teaches us to let Him lead. As our God-reliance grows, we stop needing to control our circumstances or speed through the moment to get to what we think might be better. Instead, we're content in our present moment because that's where we meet our Savior. In the present, we enter into each opportunity the Spirit gives to pour into others. Our communion with Christ shines through our souls, and the world witnesses the kind of beauty that blesses God.

Father, I'm daily bombarded with ways to achieve external beauty, but I want inner transformation instead. Please tenderize my heart to be soft and gentle in Your hands as You form Christ's character inside of me. In Jesus's name.

HOOKED ON LOVE

Be completely humble and gentle; be patient,
bearing with one another in love.

EPHESIANS 4:2 NIV

The weekend his son had been waiting for was finally here. Dad would take off from work a little early to pick up his eight-year-old from school and take him to the State Park where they planned to fish for the rest of the afternoon.

Bouncing with energy, the boy could barely sit still long enough for his dad to bait the hook. But within minutes of having his line in the water, the boy's hook got caught on an underwater tree. Cutting the hook free, the dad set up the line again. But either the fish bit the bait off the hook, the line got tangled, or the boy kept hooking various kinds of debris. Though the dad would have loved the chance to fish, too, he focused his efforts on helping his son. That night by the campfire, they cooked hot dogs in the absence of any fish. "I had a lot of fun with you today, Son," the dad affirmed, patting his boy on the back.

"Me too!" The boy smiled back and leaned against his dad's shoulder.

Good parents understand that training up children to become responsible adults takes time, strong communication, and a lot of patience. We're able to survive the setbacks and frustrations because we know they're in the growing-up process and the role we play has a strong impact on the end result. So we extend the grace they need to grow and thrive.

But God wants us to extend even greater grace—not just to the family members we love, but to everyone He places in our path and especially to those in the family of God. All of us are in the process of becoming who God designed us to be, but none of us are there yet. Setbacks, disappointment, and frustration—even in the family of God—become opportunities to humbly and gently bear each other's burdens, forgive, and forge ahead in full faith that God will finish the work He's started in each of us.

Father, thank You for your tremendous patience and gentleness toward me. You never treat me as my sins deserve. Instead, You correct and forgive and pursue me with Your goodness. Help me to extend Your kind of grace and gentleness to others. In Jesus's name.

WOOD, HAY, AND TROUBLE

But as for you, O man of God,
flee these things. Pursue
righteousness, godliness, faith, love,
steadfastness, gentleness.

I TIMOTHY 6:11 ESV

*W*hoever planned this year's Fourth of July festivities must've never had kids," one parent commented as other onlookers gathered around. As part of a weekend-long celebration, kids aged twelve and under were invited to join in the Needle in a Haystack game. More than thirty kids lined up to participate. The event organizer explained the rules: on the count of three, every kid would rush toward the stack of hay bales in the center of the field. Hidden throughout the straw they'd find coins and even dollar bills! The object, of course, was to see who could find the most money the fastest.

On the count of three, all thirty kids converged at once on the hay bales. Clawing and scratching their way toward the center, the larger kids dominated the smaller ones in pursuit of the coins. Within just a few minutes the bales had disintegrated under the frenzy, and countless children walked back, bruised and scratched, with nothing but pennies to show for the battle. Even those with a few dollar bills still left disappointed. In the end, the game proved to be both painful and pointless.

God says that the same reality applies in the larger game of life. So many people fight and claw their way to establish financial success, never noticing the collateral damage to their families, friends, and even their own souls. Fortunately, our heavenly Father wants us to experience true abundant life complete with peace and joy—the kind no amount of cash can buy. When we stop fixating on our financial situation and fix our eyes on Jesus instead, contentment and peace grow. Instead of constantly grasping for more, we discover the joy of generous living. As God meets our every need, we are freed to look out for the needs of others.

Do you ever get tired of endless competition against others? Jesus shows us the way out, through pursuing righteousness, godliness, faith, love, endurance, and gentleness—the greatest of riches that last forever.

Lord, I don't want to waste my effort on what doesn't last. Help me to make the most of my time on earth by living generously and pursuing the kind of character that pleases You most. In Jesus's name.

LEAD ME

He tends His flock like a shepherd:
He gathers the lambs in His arms
and carries them close to His heart;
He gently leads those that have young.
ISAIAH 40:11 NIV

*I*t seemed like it was just five minutes ago when she heard her baby crying. She checked her watch and realized nearly two hours had passed since the last feeding. Sighing deeply from sleep deprivation, she headed toward the crib where her crying child lay. En route to his room, she tripped over the toys her other two toddlers had left out. From the corner of her eye she spied the sink stacked high with dirty dishes, and laundry piled on the table still unfolded. She closed her eyes to shut out the failures and focused instead on her beautiful baby boy.

As she picked him up, she gently swayed to calm his sobs and soothed his concern with a warmed bottle of milk. Then cuddling him closely, she rocked him back and forth in time with the lullaby softly playing in his room. Suddenly, she realized she was singing the familiar tune, "Jesus Loves Me." The simple melody resonated with her work-weary soul and rekindled her hope. Just as her son found rest and love in her arms, God was holding and helping her. She wasn't alone, and she was deeply loved.

Even in the most ideal environment, parenting is difficult. Whether you're battling dirty diapers or navigating life-changing conversations with your teen, the challenges can seem bigger than our weary bodies can handle. Our Father in heaven isn't waiting to slam the gavel down in judgment against our weakness. Instead, He invites us into His open arms where He nourishes us and replenishes our strength through the power of His Spirit. Where we lack wisdom, He provides. When we need encouragement, He delivers. As our everlasting Shepherd, He is leading us gently, holding us close to His heart.

Lord, thank You for leading me as I seek to shepherd and lead my children to You. Your kindness and closeness give me the courage I need to keep going. In Jesus's name.

BETTER BRAKES

No discipline is enjoyable while it is happening—
it's painful! But afterward there will be
a peaceful harvest of right living for
those who are trained in this way.

HEBREWS 12:11 NLT

She stepped on the dusty scale that had sat in her bathroom untouched for months. Countless events and food-laden celebrations had come and gone through the holidays and beyond, and she had noticed the change in how her clothes felt. But yesterday after her friend sent her a recent group selfie, she moaned. Then the numbers on the scale confirmed her fears. She was heavier than she'd ever been.

Part of her wanted to go grab a tub of ice cream to console herself, but she knew that's not what she really needed. If she wanted to see change, today—right now—was the moment to begin. Establishing a new exercise routine and healthier rhythms was difficult at first, but she pressed on to increase her stamina and strength. And she started her day in prayer, asking for divine help in each of her daily decisions. Little by little, she noticed a difference. Within a month, others saw it too. It wasn't all smooth sailing from there, but she smiled knowing she was headed in a better direction.

Changing the pattern or course of our lives is challenging. Putting brakes on the bad and accelerating into a better way can feel all but impossible, especially when we've experienced failure in the past. But Scripture reminds us of a crucial truth as we seek to subdue our flesh: we don't fight against it alone! As God's kids, we have His Holy Spirit inside of our earthen, bodily vessels. He stands ready to remind us of our worth and purpose in every moment of our lives and empower us to walk in a manner worthy of the Lord.

As we grow in sensitivity to His still, small voice, we can silence the lies that have directed our errant behavior. We grow more alert to the temptations and become quicker to reach out for help, taking even our thoughts captive to make them obedient to God's Word. With each area of surrender, our old futile and fleshly patterns weaken and our spirit grows stronger, allowing more of His Spirit to pour out His blessing in and through us. Spirit-led self-control is not a destination but rather a daily opportunity to rely on God's help in the moment.

Lord, I want to feed and nourish my spirit. Help me to renew my mind according to Your Word and strengthen my physical body that I might be ready to obey Your lead today and every day. In Jesus's name.

SPECTATOR SPORTS

Everyone who competes in the games goes into strict training. They do it to get a crown that will not last, but we do it to get a crown that will last forever.

I CORINTHIANS 9:25 NIV

For weeks it was all he could talk about. Ever since his dad had taken him to see his first hockey game, the twelve-year-old boy was convinced he'd become the next all-star hockey athlete. "Why don't we start with watching some videos so you can get a feel for the rules of the sport?" his dad suggested, pleased to see his son passionate about his new pursuit. His dad sent him the links and signed him up for in-person lessons at their local ice-skating rink.

But one step onto the ice and the boy's bravery melted. After immediately falling onto his back, it took a full minute just to figure out how to stand up. Steadying himself against the wall, he tried to work his way around the rink but eventually bolted out the closest exit and removed his ice skates. "I just like watching it better," he muttered to his dad, frowning in frustration.

In a culture that sensationalizes professional athletes and musicians, it's common to covet their abilities. We dream of making it big like them if we can just get our big break too. But it's easy to overlook the years of study, preparation, and practice that brought on so much success.

The same may be even truer in spiritual matters. We say we want to be strong Christians. We hope to live a life of impact. But intimacy with God and knowledge of His ways won't happen if we don't go all in with Him, learning and applying what He says. God doesn't allow for spectator Christianity. If we intend to be true followers of Jesus, we will not only watch what He does and listen for His direction, but we will also consistently put in the work to train for success. As we build our lives on His firm foundation, we'll be ready to take on life's difficulties with His truth, grace, and power.

Lord, I admit that I've been lazy in my relationship with You, content to just get by instead of pressing in to study Your Word and walk moment by moment with You. Would you please change me and help me to obey everything You say? In Jesus's name.

UNSOUND SLUMBER

So then, let us not be like others, who are asleep, but let us be awake and sober.

I THESSALONIANS 5:6 NIV

It's not that the pew was all that comfortable. The thin pad beneath her and the hard wooden back should have kept her at attention. But before the sermon even started, she could feel fatigue setting in. The longer she sat, the heavier her eyelids became. Soon her entire focus became simply staying awake, regardless of what her pastor was saying. But the sound of his soothing voice and the silence of the room sabotaged her every effort. Her eyelids closed, and her mind wandered off into a distant land full of delightful though distorted distractions until... thud! Her head hit the back of the pew, sounding like she'd hit a home run in the middle of the church service. Instantly awake and equally embarrassed, she regained composure and focused once more on the message.

Falling asleep in inappropriate places causes problems. It can make us miss important information for a test or cause our car to run off the road. There is a time for sleep, but not in the moments when it's important to be awake!

The Bible often warns the Church about falling asleep—not the kind where your head hits the pew, but when we become spiritually lethargic in the issues that matter the most. In a culture that craves comfort, it's so easy to shift our focus to finding whatever we think will make life more pleasant and fun for us and our family. We can even look good doing it as we grow comfortable in our typical church routines.

But Jesus tells us to watch out! If we fill our lives with temporal pleasures while failing to seek the kingdom of God, it's as if we've fallen asleep in a time of war when we should've stayed strong at our post. With an enemy who's always after our demise, we can suffer much more than just embarrassment when we allow spiritual laziness to sap our zeal and deter our obedience to God's ways. But God gives us strength and the Spirit of self-control that keeps us at attention.

Father, I don't want to get lulled into following the world instead of sticking close to You. Wake me up to Your truth and give me the self-control I need to persevere in choosing what's right. In Jesus's name.

YES AND NO

God did not give us a spirit that makes us afraid
but a spirit of power and love and self-control.
II TIMOTHY 1:7 NCV

As the girl watched the video on the church's big screen, tears began to fall. She watched as missionaries in a distant land described the abject poverty around them that robbed the people they served of the very basic necessities they needed, like food and water. Comfortable in her seat, the girl focused on the images of young children playing outside in the street with something that looked like a wadded-up ball of tape. "Children turn the trash others throw out of car windows into toys that they can play with, like this makeshift ball," the missionary explained.

From her seat, she thought of all that she had to play with and how hard life must be for some other people. She tugged on her mom's sleeve. "I'm not going to buy that bike with my birthday money," she whispered, trying not to distract others in the church service. "I'm going to give it to the missionary to help the children."

"But you've been saving up for over a year," her mom said, wanting to make sure her child understood the sacrifice.

"That's okay. I can start saving again for next year," she said with an earnest smile.

Doesn't generosity make us all smile? It signals that some light still exists in an otherwise dark and self-serving world. It's also the hallmark of a surrendered heart seeking to serve others as Jesus did.

Just like the little girl, we can make better use of the time, talent, and treasure God has given to us by being a blessing to others. It's God's own Spirit inside of us cheering us on each time we trust Him by saying "No" to serving ourselves and "Yes" to prioritizing others. We do the choosing, but the Spirit inside us produces the changes. As we exercise Holy Spirit-driven self-control, we begin to curb our earthly desires and crave the values of God instead. In the process of dying to ourselves, Jesus is lifted up and draws others to Himself.

Lord, You know how strong of an urge it is to just live for myself and meet my own needs and wants. But Your way is infinitely better. Help me to discipline myself to prioritize You and the people You love. In Jesus's name.

SOUL SEWAGE

*A person without self-control is like
a city with broken-down walls.*

PROVERBS 25:28 NLT

*H*e looked at his watch impatiently, pacing back
and forth. "Why is she always late?" he vented
to the sky as he remembered other occasions where
she had held him up. Soon, other bitter thoughts
joined his frenzied thinking, and his blood began to
boil. By the time she pulled up to the curb, he could
hardly contain himself.

"How could you?" the yelling began before
she even exited the vehicle. In his direct line of fire,
she stood frozen in surprise. He unleashed every
angry thought he'd had and even invented some
accusations along the way. To hear him tell it, she
must be some kind of monster. He felt justified in
slaying the dragon.

It was then that he noticed their youngest
daughter sitting in the back seat taking it all in. "You
were supposed to drop her off!" he accused again,
confused.

"When I went to drop her off, the school's power
was off," she calmly explained. "They sent us all
home, and that's why I'm late."

Embarrassed by his outburst, he mumbled

an apology, and they went on their way. But the exchange ruined the rest of the day.

Like toothpaste squeezed out of a tube, we can't push the mess we make with our words back in after they're spoken. There's always collateral damage— not only in our relationships with others but also with God. Angry outbursts and hostile language at home, at work, and especially online cause harm to our witness when we profess to be followers of Christ. Our hostility and hypocrisy cause others to question Christianity instead of coming to Jesus. So God calls us to self-control. Before a word ever exits our mouths, He wants to be Lord of the storm brewing in our minds and hearts. His love and forgiveness can heal the bitterness that brings out the soul's sewage. But we must surrender the anger to Him first.

Do you tend to impulsively react to situations that strain your relationships? Ask God today to increase His Spirit's control over your heart and mind. Allow His peace and love to lift your thoughts to higher ground so that you can bring others to where God is.

Lord, please forgive me for the careless ways I've let my words hurt others. Help me to speak words that bring life into every situation through the power of Your Spirit. In Jesus's name.

GAME CHANGER

For this very reason, make every effort to add to your faith goodness; and to goodness, knowledge; and to knowledge, self-control; and to self-control, perseverance; and to perseverance, godliness; and to godliness, mutual affection; and to mutual affection, love. For if you possess these qualities in increasing measure, they will keep you from being ineffective and unproductive in your knowledge of our Lord Jesus Christ.

II PETER 1:5-8 NIV

*H*er daughter was staring so intently at the screen, she didn't notice her mom walk in the room and sit beside her on the sofa. The latest iteration of her favorite role-playing game had just released the day before, and the girl was already making significant progress. "Why don't you open that chest?" her mom queried as she surveyed the enchanted castle. Moving deftly around it, her daughter's avatar approached some innocent-looking flowerpots instead. Suddenly she began whacking them with her sword. "What on earth...?" the mom's voice trailed off as she watched the pots eventually explode, leaving behind a shiny, golden key.

"Now I can unlock the chest," her determined

daughter explained. "Everything builds on itself, so you have to keep gathering treasures as you go, which leads to the next treasure."

Similarly, in the Christian life, we've been given a mission. We are here on this earth to discover more about God and help the lost find Him too. Accepting Christ as our Savior isn't the end goal—it's just the beginning! Like walking through a portal, a new life focus begins once we belong to Jesus. As we go through life, God uses trials and troubles to teach us more about Him. Like the gamer daughter, we need to keep our eyes riveted on Him, ever watching for each little truth treasure He's revealing as we trust Him through whatever circumstances we face. As we follow His lead, God shows us the keys in Scripture to unlocking more truth, growing stronger in faith, overcoming sin, and loving others deeply. Through Spirit-empowered self-control, we learn to wield each gift God gives in a way that grows us up in Christ and leads us to ultimate victory at our mission's end. If we don't want to waste our time here on earth, we need to stockpile the gems of God's great character so that out of the overflow of our abundance we can seek out and share His goodness with others.

Lord, please help me add the qualities You value in my life so that I can effectively represent and serve You better. Please help me to stay focused and disciplined so that I finish well. In Jesus's name.

DYING TO LIVE

And calling the crowd to him with his disciples,
he said to them, "If anyone would come
after me, let him deny himself and
take up his cross and follow me."

MARK 8:34 ESV

*N*ews of her stage IV cancer rattled her at first. Seeking solace in her friends and family, she took a few days to process her options. None of them looked pleasant. But she knew this: she wanted to live. She wanted to keep raising her children and loving her husband and serving her church. Despite the dreadful side effects, she chose to take the treatments and fight to save her life.

And it was a struggle! Daily she battled nausea, weakness, and hair loss. Food lost its allure, and she was finding it difficult to sleep through the night. Many times she thought the chemotherapy would kill her before the cancer did. But midway through the regimen, her scan results showed tumor shrinkage. The treatment was working! It was just the encouragement she needed to continue to battle until every single cancer cell was conquered. And she won!

We cheer for cancer survivors because we know what a difficult battle they've faced. The final victory is worth the daily fight. The same is true for the Christian's fight of faith. Our sinful nature—that part of us that wants to rebel and live our own way—is like cancer to our soul and spirit. But each time we lay down our perceived rights and desires in order to follow and obey Jesus's instructions, we kill off the spiritual cancer (worldly desires) and allow healthy cells (our spirit) to grow. We get stronger in our understanding of God's ways, and our faith becomes anchored in real-life experience with Him.

The more we die to ourselves and our earthly desires, the more influence His Spirit has on our minds, in our hearts, and ultimately in the way we live.

Dying to self is a daily, often painful battle to choose God's ways over our own. But He gives us the self-control we need to choose Him again and again. As believers, we are no longer slaves to sin. We are free to grow and produce bountiful fruit that brings healing and blessing to others around us.

Lord, help me to follow Your example of total surrender and obedience to the Father. The fight is hard, but I thank You that You've given me Your Spirit to help me persevere. Use my life to bless as many people as possible. In Jesus's name.

ABOVE IT ALL

My dear brothers and sisters, take note of
this: Everyone should be quick to listen, slow
to speak and slow to become angry.

JAMES 1:19 NIV

She had been meeting with her mental health counselor for months trying to get to the bottom of her anger issues. They had surfaced first at home with her husband and kids, but now it was spilling over into her relationships at work and church too. Finally, through the course of time and careful consideration, she realized the root of her bitterness stemmed from her very strained relationship with her dad. "How can I overlook so much hurt?" she cried, wanting freedom from her bitterness.

"It's okay to acknowledge his sin and the hurt he caused," her counselor coached, "but recognize that he, too, acted that way because of pain and evil influencing him. Hurt people end up hurting people."

Suddenly, a light bulb went off. Her dad was simply a sinner like herself in need of saving grace. Understanding how much God had already forgiven her, she realized her father's debt to her was small by comparison. "I want to release him to God," she decided.

The counselor smiled. "It's not easy, but forgiveness

is the only way to real freedom."

It's easy to hold grudges and grow bitter over the various wounds others inflict on us. Our natural inclination is to want them to pay for the pain they've caused. But holding onto unforgiveness is like drinking poison to hurt someone else. We end up suffering instead.

But God's Spirit of grace gives us the self-control we need to avoid that trap. He makes us brave enough to acknowledge the pain others have caused while bringing the wound to Him for healing. Part of the process may require honest confrontation with that person, when possible. But either way, He is pleased when we release our hurt into His hands and allow His Spirit of mercy and grace to flow through us and empower us to heal and forgive. In unclogging our soul, we are set free to new and deeper levels of joy and peace in our lives. Instead of reacting in anger, we can pray for our discernment and their freedom from the enemy's deception. In praying for others who offend us, we keep the soil of our hearts fertile for further growth without any weeds of bitterness cropping up to spoil our progress.

Lord, please keep watch over the soil of my heart and let no bitter root develop there. Help me to view others through Your lens of compassion, and help me to be slow to anger and quick to forgive. In Jesus's name.

EYES ON THE PRIZE

Watch out that you do not lose what we have worked for, but that you may be rewarded fully.

II JOHN 1:8 NIV

With so many kids in her home for Vacation Bible School, she knew she needed some crowd-control strategies. So once they were all seated, she explained the rules to help the children exercise self-control. "I'm going to give each of you three stickers to put on your arm," she explained. "And here's the deal. Whoever has three stickers on their arm by the end of Bible story time will get to pick three prizes out of the treasure chest." As she revealed the golden chest full of small toys, the children squealed in delight. "But here's the catch," she continued. "If you talk or move around or make a lot of noise, I'm not going to say anything to you—but I will come over and remove one sticker." The room grew silent. Every first and second grader there understood what was at stake. With so many friends around, it was going to be super hard to stay quiet. So they kept their eyes on the prize to stay focused. By the end of the Bible story, everyone heard the message and got to pick treasures from the chest!

It's not just children who need motivation to stay on task. We all do. God understands because He made us that way, and He has provided promises far greater than Dollar Store trinkets to incentivize our faith. He wants us to fight the good fight of faith for our whole life and stay faithful all the way to the finish line—no slowing down or falling to the wayside. But like the VBS children, we are easily distracted and tempted to quit when faced with challenges. God will reward us in heaven for every eternal investment we make in His kingdom while on earth. For the believer, it's a win-win: mercy and forgiveness on this side of heaven, everlasting rewards in the life to come. May God's precious promises empower us to press on toward Jesus all the days of our lives.

God, You don't owe me anything, but I'm grateful that You notice the good works Your children do and You are faithful to reward us according to what You see. You are a good, good Father! In Jesus's name.

GENERATING HOPE

May the God of hope fill you with all joy and peace
as you trust in Him, so that you may overflow
with hope by the power of the Holy Spirit.
ROMANS 15:13 NIV

They had braced for the winter storm's impact but couldn't have guessed how dire the situation would get. Freezing rain made roadways too slick for travel, and cars caught in the downpour slid helplessly off the roads into ditches and into each other. Many had to walk to nearby businesses or homes to find shelter. But thick ice accumulation downed power lines throughout the city, cutting off power and leaving thousands without any source of heat at all. Worst of all, the forecast called for continued freezing temperatures for the next several days. Without power, heat, or open grocery stores, people remained stuck wherever they were and huddled together to stay warm.

But not everyone suffered so severely. Some had planned ahead and purchased generators for just such an occasion. When the power lines fell, they cranked on their generators that kept the power flowing. Heaters and stoves continued to work, and their homes became makeshift shelters for their neighbors who desperately needed it.

It's a picture of the secret power available to every believer that helps us weather the storms of this life and provide hope for others who need a refuge too. Our God and Father brings life-saving hope to everyone who puts their trust in Jesus, His Son. We no longer draw our power or hope from the fleeting, empty promises our culture gives. Believers become empowered from within, with the Spirit of all wisdom and power generating the kind of hope, joy, and peace that all people everywhere are desperate to find.

We have the unique opportunity to share this eternal resource with everyone God brings our way. Out of the overflow of abundance our Father lavishes on us, we are able to share the hope, love, peace, and power of God when we welcome others into our homes and lives. Today, be the generator of hope for someone in your life.

Lord, I praise You because You are the God of all hope. Simply by trusting in You, I have all the power I need to live a meaningful, purpose-filled life and to invite others in to do the same. Thank You for sending Your Spirit to light up the world! In Jesus's name.

COME!

The Spirit and the bride say, "Come."
And let the one who hears say, "Come."
And let the one who is thirsty come;
let the one who desires,
take the water of life without cost.

REVELATION 22:17 NASB

*I*t was her church's campus cleanup day, and she arrived at 8:00 a.m. sharp. "Just tell me what to do, and I'll get on it," she told the leader of the volunteer group. Soon she found herself on the far side of the property pulling weeds and picking up trash around the perimeter. By midmorning, she was already feeling the sun's heat starting to sap her energy and enthusiasm, and wondered how much longer she could continue. Just then, she looked up and noticed some of the volunteers walking with full plates of food toward the picnic tables.

"Hey, where'd you get that?" she asked.

"They sent an invite out over text," came the reply.

She looked at her phone and saw the notice: "Come inside to Room 214 for refreshments." Immediately she headed over to the designated room and opened the door to a smorgasbord of sandwiches, fruits, salads, side dishes, sodas, and a whole table dedicated to desserts. "Wow! Would you look at all this?!" she marveled at the provision. Ravenous from all her hard work, she piled her plate high. "This sure beats the water bottle I had packed." She smiled as she sat down to join the others outside.

Wouldn't it be fun if we always had a special place where we could go for refreshment, no matter what time of day it is? Well, good news: check your messages! Right now, the Holy Spirit is calling you and every person weary and war-torn from the toil and troubles of this life. Better than the offerings in Room 214, Jesus offers Himself—the Living Water and the Bread of Life that satisfies our thirsty and hungry souls forever. Today, let us come to our Father and ask for more of His precious Spirit, that we may live out our days under His divine direction and produce the fruit that feeds the nations and pleases Him.

Holy Spirit, I hear Your call, and I'm coming!
I belong to You and ask that You fill me to
overflowing with all of Your goodness and lead
me in the way everlasting. In Jesus's name.

LIVE YOUR FAITH

Dear Friend,

This book was prayerfully crafted with you, the reader, in mind. Every word, every sentence, every page was thoughtfully written, designed, and packaged to encourage you—right where you are this very moment. At DaySpring, our vision is to see every person experience the life-changing message of God's love. So, as we worked through rough drafts, design changes, edits, and details, we prayed for you to deeply experience His unfailing love, indescribable peace, and pure joy. It is our sincere hope that through these Truth-filled pages your heart will be blessed, knowing that God cares about you—your desires and disappointments, your challenges and dreams.

He knows. He cares. He loves you unconditionally.

BLESSINGS!
THE DAYSPRING BOOK TEAM

**Additional copies of this book and
other DaySpring titles can be purchased
at fine retailers everywhere.
Order online at dayspring.com
or
by phone at 1-877-751-4347**